D1097257

AMERICA'S PRINTED FABRICS
1770 - 1890

BARBARA BRACKMAN

- 8 Reproduction Quilt Projects
- Historic Notes & Photographs
- Dating Your Quilts

C&T PUBLISHING

Text and Artwork© 2004 Barbara Brackman
Artwork © 2004 C&T Publishing

Editor: Liz Aneloski
Technical Editors: Sara Kate MacFarland,
 Cynthia Keys Hilton, and Joyce Lytle
Copyeditor/Proofreader: Eva Simoni Erb/
 Carol Barrett
Cover Designer/Design Director/Book Designer:
 Kristy A. Konitzer
Illustrator: Tim Manibusan
Production Assistants: Jeff Carrillo and Luke Mulks
Photography: Jon Blumb, unless otherwise noted
Published by C&T Publishing, Inc., P.O. Box 1456,
Lafayette, California 94549
Back cover: Mary Stite's Medallion and Cactus Rose

All rights reserved. No part of this work covered by the copyright
hereon may be reproduced or used in any form or by any means—
graphic, electronic, or mechanical, including photocopying, record-
ing, taping, or information storage and retrieval systems—without
written permission of the publisher. The copyrights on individual
artworks are retained by the artists as noted in *America's Printed
Fabrics 1770–1890*.

Attention Teachers: C&T Publishing, Inc. encourages you to use
this book as a text for teaching. Contact us at 800-284-1114 or
www.ctpub.com for more information about the C&T Teachers
Program.

We take great care to ensure that the information included in this
book is accurate and presented in good faith, but no warranty is
provided nor results guaranteed. Having no control over the choic-
es of materials or procedures used, neither the author nor C&T
Publishing, Inc. shall have any liability to any person or entity with
respect to any loss or damage caused directly or indirectly by the
information contained in this book. For your convenience, we
post an up-to-date listing of corrections on our website
(www.ctpub.com). If a correction is not already noted, please contact our customer service department at ctinfo@ctpub.com or at
P.O. Box 1456, Lafayette, California 94549.

Trademarked (™) and Registered Trademark (®) names are used
throughout this book. Rather than use the symbols with every
occurrence of a trademark and registered trademark name, we are
using the names only in the editorial fashion and to the benefit of
the owner, with no intention of infringement.

Brackman, Barbara.
 America's printed fabrics 1770-1890 : 8 reproduction quilt
projects;
historic notes & photographs; dating your quilts / Barbara
Brackman.
 p. cm.
 ISBN 1-57120-255-2 (Paper trade)
1. Patchwork--United States--Patterns. 2. Quilting--United
States--Patterns. 3. Textile fabrics. 4. Quilts--United
States--Dating. 5. Quilts--United States--Identification. I. Title.
TT835.B63636 2004
746.46'041'0973--dc22
                              2003026875

Printed in China

10 9 8 7 6 5 4 3 2 1

Acknowledgments

*I am a woman who is quite fortunate in my friends,
as you will see from the quilts in this book. I sew
with two groups each Thursday, the "Sew Whatevers"
in the morning and the "Women Who Run With
Scissors" in the afternoon. Each group is supportive,
inspirational, and remarkably prolific. I want to
thank those women who've loaned their quilts for this
book: Shauna Christensen, Georgann Eglinski, Pam
Mayfield, Karla Menaugh, Cherié Ralston, Roseanne
Smith, Jean Stanclift, Terry Thompson, and Shirlene
Wedd. Other friends who I don't get to see as regularly also loaned quilts for photography: Bobbi Finley,
Carol Jones, Jo Morton, Judy Severson, and Penny
Tucker. I'm grateful to the quilters—Shirley
Greenhoe, Lori Kukuk, Pam Mayfield, Rosie
Mayhew, and Anne Thomas—who always make
time to finish the quilts in style. And thanks to the
Harwood and Jackson families who loaned antique
quilts for photography. I have a terrific collection of
antique cottons, most of which were given to me by
my good friend Joyce Gross. I also want to thank
Terry Thompson, who is so generous with her impres-
sive swatch collection, and Mary Sue Hannan, Pat
Nikols, Bets Ramsey, Arnold Savage, and Mary
Williams, who, over the years, have sent scraps they
thought I might like. Without the fabric, there'd be no
book. As always, thanks to Jon Blumb, who photographs the quilts so expertly, and editor Liz Aneloski,
who pulls it all together.*

Contents

Introduction

Quilts grow out of available fabric. They are truly the art of the found object, the object being yard goods. Unless she can dye, print, or weave her own, the quiltmaker relies on what's fashionable, practical, and still on the shelves. We have an incredible variety of cottons printed and dyed just for quilts. Among the millions of bolts manufactured each season are reproduction prints that accurately echo the fabric of the past.

The purpose of this book is twofold: to give you insight into how fabric has affected the look of the nineteenth-century American quilt, and to show you how to use today's reproductions to interpret antique quilts.

This book relies a bit on textile science, but it is primarily a book by a connoisseur, a quiltmaker with a good eye. Dating quilts is more a matter of art than science, a matter of looking and matching, categorizing and recalling. You may also be a quilt connoisseur ("one who knows" in French). If not yet, I hope this book will help train your eye in recognizing fabrics and quilt style.

Train your eye by looking and remembering, by collecting fabric and pictures of fabric, new and old, and by making copies of antique quilts. Begin with a close copy of a scrappy old quilt, matching reproduction fabrics to each antique swatch not only to study fabric, but also to understand how women sorted their scraps and thought about symmetries and color. A few reproduction quilts here are close copies of the originals; more are updated versions inspired by the past.

This is a how-to book in many ways. The detailed instructions for projects inspired by nineteenth-century quilts will teach skills in imitating quilt style

and dating antique fabrics it's also a how-to book on shopping. You'll learn skills in identifying reproductions, and in determining what fabric the designer is attempting to copy. Right here I'm giving you a license to buy the reproductions when you see them. How much? A fat quarter if it's any accurate reproduction; five yards if it's a great pillar print that might make a good border. Make yourself a checklist of fabric styles, and be sure you've got a stash of each type.

I've included quotations from old diaries, letters, newspapers, and catalogs to give you insight into the role of fabric and quilts in people's lives. I've also included photographs of people wearing the prints we see in the quilts of the times. I've identified photographs using technical names for photography processes, so it may help to know something of photography's technological timeline. My earliest photos, dating to the 1850s, include ambrotypes and tintypes printed on glass or metal. Early paper photographs, small portraits called *carte de visites* (French for "visiting cards") appeared just before the Civil War and remained popular through century's end. Cabinet cards mounted on heavier paper were the most common photos in the 1880s and 1890s. In those years, stereographs or stereo cards were parlor entertainment. Two slightly different shots printed side by side appear three-dimensional through a viewer. Bedrooms and factories were both common subjects, so we can study interior decoration and fabric technology from stereo cards. Postcards and snapshots appeared about 1900, giving us informal glimpses of people in their work and play clothing.

An asterisk by a reproduction quilt means the quiltmaker has published pattern instructions. Look in the Resource List for ordering information.

Block-printed chintzes in a variety of colored blotch grounds with a possible toile at the top. Between a cross-stitched pocket book by Cherié Ralston and a recent wood block from India is a reproduction silhouette portrait.

CHAPTER I

The Fabric of the Revolution
1770 - 1820

PENNSYLVANIA, FEBRUARY 27, 1793

" *A Citizen Presents to the Consort of our most worthy President; a piece of elegant Chintz, the fabrick of which was imported from India, in an American [ship]; and printed by the subscriber in his manufactory....It is presumed if the worthy person here address'd, would honor the manufacture of our own country so far as to wear a dress made of the piece accompanying this; it... would help remove the prejudice, that at present too much prevails against American manufactures.* "

LETTER FROM JOHN HEWSON TO MARTHA WASHINGTON[1]

The Quilts

*Reproduction wallhanging, patchwork portrait of George Washington, detail, by Karla Menaugh, 2002, Lawrence, Kansas, wool appliqué on cotton.

The quilt, the quintessential American folk art, shares a common history with our country. As the colonists developed a hunger for American independence, they developed an American quilt style. American patchwork quilts date to the 1770s, the decade we gained freedom from England's rule. While Bostonians rebelled against taxes on tea and Virginians called a Continental Congress, colonial needlewomen created a fashion for cutting up imported chintzes and refashioning them into patchwork bedcovers.

Earlier American quilts were what we call wholecloth. Backing and batting were topped by a single piece of fabric embellished with quilting designs that also functioned to secure the layers together. In her will, Virginian Mary Washington left such a

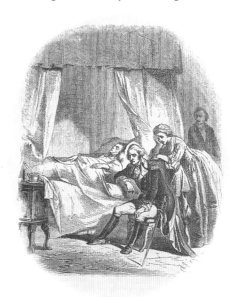

Mid-nineteenth-century wood engraving of George and Martha Washington at the deathbed of their son. Draped beds were the standard furniture of the period.

motifs from printed cottons are rearranged on a plain piece of fabric in a new composition. Pieced quilts featured simple triangle or star designs, usually set with a central focus, what we call a medallion. Only two of eleven date-inscribed quilts from this era were based on the grid or block-style format that became the standard set for patchwork quilts in the nineteenth century.[5]

Characteristics of the earliest patchwork quilts include a central design focus, or medallion set, and a mixture of fibers. Nineteenth-century quiltmakers might decide to make a cotton quilt, but eighteenth-century women stitched patches of wool, silk, linen, and cotton into the same piece. When quiltmakers did confine their scrapbag to the cellulosic fibers—cotton and linen—they mixed print scale. Large-scale furnishing fabric called chintz was often combined with the smaller-scale dress prints often called calico.

Antique whole-cloth quilt (detail) made by Sarah Smith, Catherine Smith, and Hannah Callender, 1761, Philadelphia. Collection of Independence National Historical Park. Three Quaker women worked together on this light-blue silk quilt, one of the few surviving American quilts from the Colonial era. Along the top is inscribed in the quilting: "Drawn by Sarah Smith. Stiched (sic) by Hannah Callender and Catherine Smith in Testimony of their Friendship. 10 mo 5th 1761." Their neighbor Elizabeth Sandwith Drinker, a voluminous diarist, often mentioned the Smith sisters and Hannah Callender. "August 6, 1759. Spent the afternoon at Uncle Jervis's, helped to quilt—H Callender called this evening."[2]

Antique cutout chintz quilt (details), estimated date 1800-1820, possibly Maryland, Virginia Tidewater area.

Reproduction quilt, cut-out chintz appliqué by Shirley and Shirlene Wedd, 1996–1997, Lawrence, Kansas, 41" x 41". This mother/daughter team copied a chintz quilt made by Martha Bullock (1815–1896) of Greensboro, Alabama, who donated chintz quilts to Confederate fundraising fairs during the Civil War. The Wedds used an English chintz copied from a quilt made by Jane Austen. They cut the center basket directly from the fabric and fashioned wreaths of other florals in the print. [4]

piece, a "quilted blue-and-white quilt," to her son George.[3]

Several pieced or appliquéd quilts inscribed with dates from 1770 to 1800 survive. The favored appliqué technique was what we call *Broderie Perse* (Persian Embroidery) or cut-out chintz, in which

The Fabrics

Taste may have dictated how a quilt-maker arranged her blocks, but technology and trade determined the fabrics available to her. Fabric was expensive in the Revolutionary era and the early years of the United States. In 1798, when workers' wages were counted in pennies, Abigail Adams, the President's wife, wrote of paying $6 a yard for

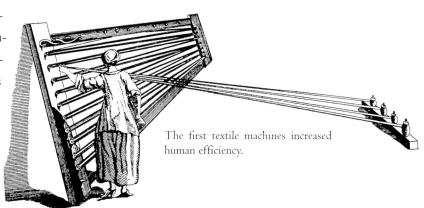

The first textile machines increased human efficiency.

fine cotton to make a fashionable white mob cap. The muslin, probably imported from India, was so outrageously expensive that she impolitely told her sister exactly what she paid.[6]

Fabric was a luxury because processing common natural fibers—wool, silk, cotton, and linen—involved much handwork. Transportation added costs, as ships navigating oceans and caravans crossing deserts carried raw materials and finished goods. Fabric production was an international business. Skilled hands in India spun fine white cottons that might be finished by calico printers in the Netherlands or

Stereograph, Lawrence Mills, Lowell, Massachusetts, about 1900. A century after America began to mechanize fabric production, the Lawrence Mills housed 330,000 spindles spinning cotton yarn to be woven into cloth. Belts that ran to a power source, the Merrimack River, powered the spindles. The noise was deafening. Here, factory workers check for empty bobbins and broken yarns.

England. Silk yarns, hand pulled from the cocoons of Chinese silkworms, were woven by French artisans into patterned brocades and damasks for European royalty.

Fabric production was the focus of the Industrial Revolution, as inventors sought to remove the skilled human hand and limited human energy from processing cloth. Early machinery such as the spinning jenny, which came into use in the 1760s, merely made human spinners more efficient, enabling an individual to fill eight or eighty spindles rather than one. A decade later, the Arkwright "Water Frame" transferred the power source, replacing muscle power with a running river. By the end of the 1780s, mechanized water-powered systems for weaving began to eliminate the need for trained artisans. Carding, cleaning, spinning, weaving, dyeing, and printing cloth would soon be the province of factories rather than households or cottage industries. Factories employing unskilled, underpaid workers replaced crafts that had fueled prosperous economies all over the world. Textile prices dropped accordingly. By 1833, Elizabeth Hodgdon recorded paying $1.12 for eight yards of calico, probably spun, woven, and printed in a New England factory.[7]

" The other day my husband went to a 'sheep shearing' . . . All the guests were asked to come dressed in American-made clothes. The wine had been made in Virginia, as were all the beverages—apple brandy, peach brandy, whiskey, etc. It was a completely patriotic fete. "

LETTER FROM ROSALIE STIER CALVERT[8]

The English Crown, hoping to maintain high fabric prices, saw the Colonial role quite clearly. Americans were to produce raw materials, such as indigo and grain, to be shipped to England, where crops were processed into finished goods, such as cloth and whiskey. The finished goods were shipped back to the colonies, to be purchased or bartered for more raw materials. To keep the colonists as perpetual customers, rather than competing manufacturers, the Crown refused them access to the tools of the Industrial Revolution. When English printer John Hewson emigrated to Philadelphia in the early 1770s, he smuggled both the machinery parts and the engineering knowledge he needed to manufacture chintzes and calicoes. Even after the English gave up trying to subdue the rebellious colonies, they embargoed trade in knowledge and machinery. In 1789, weaver Samuel Slater arrived in America with plans for Arkwright's water-powered equipment committed to memory, the only place he could carry the knowledge out of England.

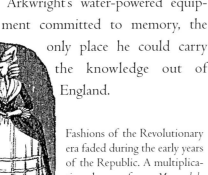

6 times 8 are 48.

DearAunt,yourdressisoutofdate.

Fashions of the Revolutionary era faded during the early years of the Republic. A multiplication lesson from *Marmaduke Multiply's Merry Method of Making Minor Mathematicians,* printed about 1815, ridicules the out-of-date look.

Postcard, 1908. Women model dresses once worn by Christiana Clinton; according to the note on the reverse, one of the models was an ancestor. The dresses appear to date from mid- to late-eighteenth century when split skirts revealed fancy petticoats, often of quilted silk. Apparently, the inherited dresses did not include the undergarments necessary to structure the stylish wide silhouette.

Late eighteenth-century woodblock prints. Floral sprigs and leafy abstractions have always been popular subject matter for prints.

LEFT: Antique quilt, *Princess Feather* by Mary Somerville (1801–?), embroidered date, May 26, 1818. Collection of Helen F. Spencer Museum of Art at the University of Kansas. Gift of Dorothy Jewell Sanders. RIGHT: *Reproduction quilt, *Princess Victoria's Feather*, designed by Barbara Brackman, appliquéd by Jean Pearson Stanclift, 2001, Lawrence, Kansas, 76" x 76". Machine quilted by Pamela Mayfield. When fabric is in the design process, printers provide designers with strike-offs, which are checked for printing errors and color. The printer revises the job as needed. Jean made the center panel from the strike-offs for a line Terry Clothier Thompson and I named for Queen Victoria. We had only small pieces of any particular print, except the botanical chintz border, so the quilt has the scrappy look often seen in early quilts, when cotton prints were expensive. We can update the look of old quilts by choosing favorite elements. Mary's quilt has too much going on for our modern taste. We borrowed a few of her best ideas, the large feather and the outside border leaves.

American resentment over English control of textile trade and technology fueled revolutionary ideas. Foreign fabrics became a symbol of English tyranny, and patriotic rebels dressed in homemade fabric—homespun wools of rural life and manufactured cottons from Philadelphia and Boston. The Industrial Revolution increased the availability of fabric, while the American Revolution encouraged a domestic American textile industry. It is certainly no coincidence that the American patchwork quilt developed during revolutionary times.

" JULY 17, 1800

I must again trouble my Dear Mother by requesting her to send on my spotted muslin . . . so long a visit in Wicassett will oblige me to muster all my muslins, for I am informed they are so monstrous smart as to take no notice of any lady that can condescend to wear a calico gown. "

LETTER FROM ELIZA SOUTHGATE[9]

CHINTZ

A fascination with chintz characterizes early quilts. The word "chintz" is related to the Hindu words for "spotted" or "painted." Historically, chintz meant a large-scale furnishing print of cotton or linen, or a combination fabric of both yarns called fustian, popular for bed drapery, quilts, curtains, and upholstery from 1700 to 1860. Many pieces had a glazed surface of wax, resin, or starch rubbed onto the fabric with a stone. The glaze helped repel stains and dirt, but washed out.

Textile historian Jeremy Adamson notes botanical chintzes were quite popular in mid-eighteenth-century England, quoting Godfrey Smith's 1756 book, *The Laboratory or School of Arts*: "The fashion of latephas run upon natural flowers, stalks, and leaves . . . sometimes in groups or festoons of flower

Robert Furber's floral catalog for July from *Twelve Months of Flowers*, 1730.

making identification of specific plants a problem in many of the old botanical chintzes.

Botanicals are an enormous class of prints—really any print, any scale, with accurate (or seemingly accurate) florals. Their polar opposite is the "ditsy" print; indeterminate flowers, cookie-cutter blossoms, stereotypical leaves, or stylized figures that vaguely resemble plant life. Susan Meller and Joost Elffers, in their 1991 book, *Textile Designs: Two Hundred Years of European Patterns*, use the terms "ditsies" and "dumb-dumbs," twentieth-century American textile jargon for inoffensive floral prints that always sell well.[11]

and fruit, and sometimes in sprigs and branches carelessly flung, ranged or dispersed in a natural and agreeable manner."[10]

The English have long been known for their love of gardening. Londoner Robert Furber is credited with printing the world's first seed catalog. Prints from his book *Twelve Months of Flowers*, published in 1730, are still popular for decorating. Such botanical studies inspired textile designers, who rendered detailed blossoms, leaves, and fruit. Details might be accurate but designers grafted fruit to flower with their pens,

The passion for chintz inevitably became passé. In 1851, English female novelist George Eliot described a room with a "chintzy and unbecoming" effect, as chintz became synonymous with bad taste and second-rate goods in Europe. America, lagging behind in fashion, maintained a taste for chintz quilts through the Civil War. After 1865, large-scale furnishing fabrics disappeared from quilters' patch bags. Calico became king.[12]

Remembering Sulgrave, reproduction top by Penelope Tucker, 2003, San Jose, California. Sulgrave is George Washington's ancestral home in England. Penny wanted to evoke the look of the American Colonial quilt and its English counterpart. White is usually a neutral in quilt color schemes, but here it pops out as a bright color.

Reproduction quilt, *Tree of Life*, hand appliquéd by Judy Severson, 1998, Belvedere, California, 91" x 91". Machine quilted by Shirley Greenhoe. Photograph by Sharon Risedorph. Judy's inspiration was the Indian Palampore, the hand-painted cotton panel traditionally used for hangings and bedcovers in India. In the late seventeenth century, thousands of Palampores were exported to Europe. Their centralized tree-of-life motif remained popular with Europeans and Americans through the early nineteenth century. The appliquéd border is cut as it was printed in a botanical chintz, modified only slightly to fit Judy's format, and enhanced with butterflies cut from several prints. She constructed her central tree of the flowers from two reproduction chintzes. Judy's update of the old *Broderie Perse* technique includes increasing symmetry and balance, and adds more flowers for a lusher look.

Antique fabric, botanical chintzes from 1790–1820. Large-scale fabrics with detailed florals are popular furnishing fabrics across the centuries. These pieces show various blotch grounds in tea (tan), dark brown, and madder red. Note the registration problems inherent in printing backgrounds with block printing technology. Halos around the figures and overlapping color add to the period look. The leafy shades of green were overprinted blue and yellow. The tea-ground fabrics look to be printed with a combination of copper roller printing and woodblocks for added color. The red and dark brown fabrics are woodblock prints, possibly with hand-applied penciling for blues and greens.

Reproduction fabric, botanical chintz prints. Today's printers often correct registration errors that make chintzes look authentic. Although printed by modern screen technology, the blue-ground chintz features halos characteristic of old woodblock grounds. The print size has been reduced but the coloring is an authentic touch. Botanicals may be renderings of roses and other European garden flowers, or of the exotic flora typical of Jacobean design (top left). Named after King James I, Jacobean design includes fanciful flowers imitating English needlework stylish from 1650 to 1850.

TOILES OR PLATE PRINTS

Toile (pronounced *twahl*) is the French word for cloth. We define toiles today as monochromatic line drawings of large-scale figures, especially botanicals and genre scenes (scenes of people at play or work). The earlier pieces were often printed on a coarse cotton, linen, or fustian. Because plates were large, the design repeat is large, measuring about 20 to 36 inches. After the invention of roller printing in the 1790s, printers copied the toile look with rollers and a smaller repeat of about 15 inches.

" *How many passages of my life seem to be epitomized in this patchwork quilt. Here is the piece intended for the centre; a star as I called it; the rays of which are remnants of that bright copperplate cushion which graced my mother's easy chair.* "

Memoir by a mill girl, 1845[13]

In the original toiles, natural dyes limited the color range. Grounds were white (blue was one exception). Figures were colored with madder-dyed shades of browns, reds, pinks, and purples. Blue toiles often featured indigo grounds with white lines. Blue lines on white grounds were probably Prussian blue. Because printers could not use two-color printing with this technique they could not print blue over yellow to make green. Black was not used, because there was no true, fast black for cotton at that point.

The look of toile grew out of the technology, an intaglio printing process just like etchings printed on paper. Intaglio (pronounced in-tall´-yo) is a negative printing technique. Ink or mordant for the dye is forced into grooves on a copper plate. Paper or fabric is applied to the plate with a good deal of pressure and the chemical is transferred to form a fine line drawing. In paper etchings or engravings the process is finished at this point, but mordant-dyed fabric must be dipped into a bath of coloring agent. Color adheres to mordanted lines and washes out of other areas. The technique is complex, requiring sophisticated knowledge of dye chemistry, and familiarity with engineering techniques necessary for the proper printing press.

France, like England in the early eighteenth century, enforced laws forbidding domestic cotton printing, hoping to protect domestic silk and wool industries. By mid-century, when regimes realized that outlawing fashionable cottons was misguided, no one in France understood modern printing methods. About 1760, the French court invited two Swiss brothers, textile printers Christophe-Phillipe and Frederic Oberkampf, to establish a plant near the court at Versailles in a town called Jouy-en-Josas. Most of the Oberkampfs' cottons were printed with woodblocks in a variety of natural dyes, but the factory at Jouy is primarily remembered for perfecting the new technology of copper-plate printing. Although other European factories printed with copper-plates, the term Toiles de Jouy (fabric from Jouy) came to describe it all.

The Oberkampf factory, which survived into the 1840s, printed the signature toiles between 1770 and 1818. Once they established the style, however, other mills continued the look, eventually using copper rollers and, in the twentieth century, silk-screen prints. Americans included toiles in their quilts from the late eighteenth century through 1860 or so, but as time went by the pieces grew smaller, while quiltmakers recycled old-fashioned toile bed-hangings down to the very last scraps.

Shopping List for Fabric of the Revolution

♦ Chintz   ♦ Botanicals   ♦ Toile

Learning Lessons From the Past

Medallion Format. The majority of quilts surviving from the first fifty years of American patchwork are composed of borders framing a central design.

Simple Pattern/Complex Fabric. Quiltmakers were fascinated with pattern and loved working with large-scale fabrics. Their quilts achieve a pleasant balance because patchwork was simple enough to allow pattern in the fabric to dominate.

Low Contrast. Quiltmakers did not focus on dark and light contrast. They enjoyed placing busy prints of the same value right next to each other.

Occasionally the viewer has a hard time figuring out just where the seams are.

Order or Chaos? Chintz quilts have little of the orderly, neat look that later quiltmakers prized, but that's their appeal. Decide on your own personal tolerance for pandemonium in quilt design. If you like a busy look, use lots of large-scale prints. Don't worry about dark and light contrast and don't worry too much about symmetry—whether pattern repeats in an orderly fashion. Symmetry just wasn't important in the quilts of the Revolution.

Rosanne's Quilt

Roseanne Smith updated the look with her four-block variation of the project quilt beginning on page 18. She used sharper contrast between lights and darks, more symmetry in the coloring, and fussy cutting of many of the large-scale prints (the term today's quilters use for isolating individual design motifs), a technique not often practiced before 1925. She added two small inner borders to define and frame the composition, a design idea quite popular at the turn of the twenty-first century.

Roseanne limited her fabrics to 3 or 4 lights and 3 or 4 darks. She sewed 4 star blocks (24" x 24" each), turned the pieced border into sashing (12 sections 6" x 24" finished), and added 3 unpieced borders (1½" finished red inner border, ¾" finished dark middle border, and 9" finished chintz outer border).

There are 9 setting blocks pieced of (A) and (B) in the center of each star just like the squares.

Reproduction quilt, *Mary Stites's Medallion* by Roseanne Smith, 2002, Lawrence, Kansas, 88½" x 88½"

Antique fabric and a block in copper-plate-printed furnishing fabrics, known as toiles, about 1790–1820. At lower left, a floral print with classical acanthus leaves, a design convention that goes back to the Greeks. The block is pieced of a madder-style roller print edged by triangles cut from a toile featuring country people at work in exotic Chinese-style hats. *Chinoiserie*, borrowing from Asian design, was fashionable at the turn of the nineteenth century.

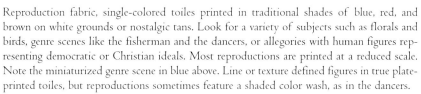

Reproduction fabric, single-colored toiles printed in traditional shades of blue, red, and brown on white grounds or nostalgic tans. Look for a variety of subjects such as florals and birds, genre scenes like the fisherman and the dancers, or allegories with human figures representing democratic or Christian ideals. Most reproductions are printed at a reduced scale. Note the miniaturized genre scene in blue above. Line or texture defined figures in true plate-printed toiles, but reproductions sometimes feature a shaded color wash, as in the dancers.

Mary Stites's Medallion

Reproduction quilt, *Mary Stites's Medallion* by Barbara Brackman, 2002, Lawrence, Kansas, 48" x 48". Machine quilted by Pamela Mayfield. I featured a toile that I redrew for Moda from a 1780s allegorical plate print honoring Benjamin Franklin and George Washington. The reproduction toile has a nostalgic tan ground rather than the white of the original. I mixed tans and whites with abandon, trying to capture the look one finds in old quilts in which the whites fade to different values.

A medallion is the perfect pattern for chintzes and toiles. Large pieces show fabric to good advantage. This medallion, the single star, is drawn from a quilt inscribed in cross-stitch "1804." The name "Mary Stites" is inked—probably after the invention of ink that wouldn't rot fabric in the 1830s. Nancy and Donald Roan, historians of southeastern Pennsylvania's Goschenhoppen region's folk culture, published this quilt in their book Lest I Shall Be Forgotten. Made in Northhampton County, Pennsylvania, it is, they believe, the earliest dated Pennsylvania-German quilt yet found.[14]

Mary's is a simple, well-balanced design, based on just seven pattern pieces. She carefully shaded lights and darks, combining dress-scale calicoes with larger chintz-scale florals. I reduced her full-size bed quilt by one quarter to make a wall quilt. Roseanne Smith multiplied my pattern four times to make a bed quilt.

FINISHED QUILT, 48" X 48"   CENTER STAR BLOCK, 24" X 24" FINISHED   BORDERS, 6" FINISHED
PIECED AND PLAIN

FABRIC REQUIREMENTS

Early quilts were scrappy, so you want to mix and match prints. I focused on browns and blues, the most common fabrics at the time. Instead of quarter yard pieces, you can buy fat quarters (18" x 22"). If you feature a toile in the center and corner squares, you'll want to fussy cut a portrait or scene.

Blues: ¼ yard each of 2 fabrics (fat quarters are fine)

Browns: ¼ yard each of 6-10 fabrics

Tans and/or other lights: ¼ yard each of 6-10 fabrics

Toile: ½ yard

Outer border: 1½ yards

Backing: 3 yards

Batting: 54" x 54"

Binding: ½ yard

CUTTING

• Cut 1 toile square and 12 brown squares 4¾" x 4¾" (A).

• Cut 2 brown and 4 light squares 3⅞" x 3⅞". Cut each in half diagonally (B).

• Cut 4 brown squares 3½" x 3½" (C).

• Cut 3 brown and 8 light squares 7¼"x 7¼". Cut each in quarters diagonally (D).

• Cut 4 light squares 6⅞" x 6⅞". Cut each in half diagonally (E).

• Cut 1 blue square 13¼" x 13¼". Cut in quarters diagonally (F).

• Cut 4 toile and 4 blue squares 6½" x 6½" (G).

• Cut 2 strips 6½" x 36½" for side borders, and 2 strips 6½" x 48½" for top and bottom borders.

For backing, trim selvages and cut the yardage into 2 pieces, each 54" long. Stitch together lengthwise and trim to fit the quilt top, leaving 2" on each side.

THE QUILT TOP

Center Block

1. Sew 4 triangles (B) to 1 square (A).

2. Add 2 star points (B) to 4 triangles (D). Make 4 rectangles. Sew 2 rectangles to opposite sides of the center square.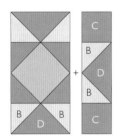

Center Unit

3. Sew squares (C) to each end of the remaining 2 rectangles (B/D/B). Add side strips to the center unit, as shown, making a star that finishes to 12".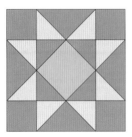

Center Star

4. Sew 2 triangles (E) to the sides of 1 triangle (F). Make 4 rectangles (E/F/E).

5. Sew 2 rectangles (E/F/E) to the top and bottom of the star.

6. Add squares (G) to the ends of the remaining 2 rectangles to make 2 strips.

7. Sew these strips to the sides of the star. You now have a larger star, 24" finished.

Head Borders

1. Sew 10 triangles (D) to 3 squares (A) as shown. Make 4 border strips 6" x 24" finished.

Completed 24" Star

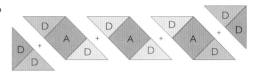

2. Add top and bottom borders to large star unit.

3. Sew squares (G) to each end of the remaining 2 borders to make strips 6" x 36" finished. Sew the strips to the sides of the quilt top.

4. Add side borders and finish with top and bottom borders.

Quilting

Pumpkin Seed Quilting Diagram

1. Mark the quilt. During the Revolutionary era, before factory-spun cotton thread was available in the 1790s, quilting was rather minimal. Thread spun from silk, wool, or linen did not encourage fancy designs in cotton quilts. Whether machine quilting or hand quilting your medallion, you'll want a utilitarian design. Pamela Mayfield outlined the central star in variations of what is still called "elbow quilting" in the South. She quilted a pumpkin seed design in the pieced border, and finished with a meandering line following the print in the outside border.

2. Layer and baste (page 125).

3. Quilt by hand or machine.

4. Bind the quilt (page 126).

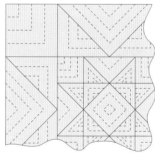
Elbow Quilting Diagram

[1] Joseph E. Fields, *Worthy Partner: The Papers of Martha Washington* (Westport, CT: Greenwood Press, 1994) Pp. 245-246.

[2] Elaine Forman Crane, *The Diary of Elizabeth Drinker*, Vol. I (Boston: Northeastern University Press, 1991) Pg. 26.

[3] The Will of Mary Washington, Fredericksburg, Virginia, May 20, 1788.

[4] Bryding Adams, "Alabama's Gunboat Quilts," *Uncoverings 1987*, Volume 8 (San Francisco, American Quilt Study Group, 1989).

[5] Barbara Brackman, *Clues in the Calico* (McLean, VA: EPM, 1989) Pg. 123.

[6] Stewart Mitchell, *New Letters of Abigail Adams* (Boston: Houghton Mifflin, 1947) Pg. 173.

[7] Thomas Dublin, *Farm to Factory* (New York: Columbia University, 1981) Pp. 55-57.

[8] Margaret Law Callcott, *Mistress of Riverdale: The Plantation Letters of Rosalie Stier Calvert* (Baltimore: Johns Hopkins University, 1991) Pg. 206.

[9] Eliza Southgate Bowne, *A Girl's Life Eighty Years Ago* (New York: Scribner's, 1887) Pp. 28-29.

[10] Jeremy Adamson, *Calico and Chintz* (Washington: Renwick Gallery, 1996) Pg. 31.

[11] Susan Meller and Joost Elffers, *Textile Designs* (New York: Abrams, 1991) Pg. 51.

[12] Letter from Eliot quoted in *Oxford English Dictionary* (Oxford: Clarendon Press, 1989).

[13] "Looking Back", *Lowell Offering*, Volume 5, 1845, Pp. 201-203.

[14] Nancy and Donald Roan, *Lest I Shall Be Forgotten: Anecdotes and Traditions of Quilts* (Green Lane, PA, Goschenhoppen Historians, 1993) Pg. 24.

A mix of old and new—antique books, a fashion plate, a schoolgirl landscape, and old chintzes on an empire-style bureau. Reproductions include china, silver, and the quilt on the wall by Carol Gilham Jones. Quilts in the drawer are antique; the feathered star on the right is inscribed 1837 in the quilting; the fringed pillow sham inscribed McM dates to the years between 1800 and 1840.

CHAPTER 2

Fabric of the Rising Sun
1820-1840

Women picking cotton as free labor about 1900. Cotton and slavery were so tightly woven that Quakers and other abolitionists refused to wear cotton before the Civil War.

Many images symbolize America—the eagle, the federal shield, Miss Liberty, and Uncle Sam. In the early days of the Republic, new citizens thought of her as a Rising Sun among nations, a model democracy that would soon ascend to the center of the international constellation.

At the dawn of the new nation, textile production enabled America to compete in the world market. Although wool and linen remained the province of Great Britain and silk the specialty of China and France, America soon assumed the role of leader in world cotton production.

LOUISIANA, APRIL 12, 1835

" I must request the favor of you to add twenty-eight yards of cheap calico in your memorandum for me. Please let it be gay. I have always given a dress of such to every woman after having a young child. I am now in debt to four that has young babes. "

PLANTATION OWNER RACHEL O'CONNOR WRITING ABOUT CLOTHING FOR HER SLAVES.[1]

American textile manufacturers spent much of the first 50 years of independence attempting to import British spinning, weaving, and printing technology, but in those years Americans also developed their reputation as innovators. In 1793, Eli Whitney developed a saw-gin, a cotton engine, to separate the seeds for short-staple cotton. His mechanical device improved the processing of cotton to such a degree that the crop became the early basis of American wealth. In 1807 America maintained 15 cotton processing mills; by 1830 there were 800.[2]

It is important to remember that very few of these early domestic textile mills printed the chintzes and calicoes we see in American quilts before 1840. Many factories specialized only in mechanically spun cotton yarn, sold to home weavers who combined

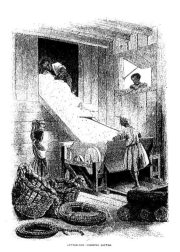

Slaves working a cotton gin, wood engraving from *Harper's Monthly*, March, 1854.

Stereograph, steamboats loading cotton bales in New Orleans, about 1900.

the cotton with homespun woolens for homewoven jeans, linseys, and other combination cloth. Homewoven cloth, while common during these decades, was rarely made entirely of cotton.

Other mills bought factory-spun cotton yarn and wove rather coarse cloth, such as cotton duck for sails or osnaburg for sacking to ship grain. In 1814, as America again waged war with England, Americans took pride in a new factory in Waltham, Massachusetts, that was the first in the United States, if not the world, to mechanically process raw cotton into woven cloth at a single site. The cloth was described as "heavy unbleached sheetings . . . a class of goods, which under the name of 'domestics,' have ever since formed the staple of American cotton manufactures." That coarse white cotton was commonly used for quilt backs, fabric that is often mistakenly called "homespun" today because of its rough look.[3]

A few artisans in Philadelphia and Rhode Island printed patterns on a finer cotton, usually imported as cloth from India. Their establishments might be called cottage industries rather than factories, because they used the age-old hand printing technology of wooden blocks. It wasn't until 1826 that British emigrant John D. Prince engineered the first American factories for cottons printed by machines using sophisticated dye chemistry and English and European technologies for roller printing.

Blotch Grounds

Printed fabrics consist of figure and ground. We classify prints primarily by figure, such as *sporting prints* with horseshoes and oars or *floral trails* with vines and blooms. We can also classify prints by their background. Grounds may be plain with just the white of the bleached cotton showing through, but grounds are more often dyed. Today's printing technology easily allows designers to give us solid-colored grounds, the common style on the bolts in our quilt shops. In the past, grounds were often more complex due to the dictates of both technology and taste.

Hand printing with woodblocks was effective for small areas of color in the figures, but selectively

Print on paper made from the woodblock on page 5. This particular block, one of a set, colors the figures. Another block would have defined lines that remain white here. A third might have dyed the background. Imagine the difficulties lining up or registering three colors applied by three different blocks.

"The Calico Printer" taps woodblocks with a mallet to decorate yardage. Repeat in a woodblock print was rather small, as the blocks measure slightly larger than a man's hand. From *The Book of Trades*, 1807. Smithsonian Institution Negative 55511

dyeing large areas of background using a wooden surface was a challenge. Printers realized that shapes of felt could be attached to blocks to print uniform colored grounds. The felt shape was called the blotch, and the chintz prints dyed with them have "blotch grounds." Blotch-ground chintzes were very popular from about 1790 through 1830, and we see scraps of them in quilts through 1860.

Blotch backgrounds appear in brown, blue, green, dark red, and yellow. Browns were most popular, either the dark brown of "dark ground prints" or the medium brown of "tea" or "tan blotch ground" prints. Dark browns were usually madder dyes, one reason dark ground prints are so likely to deteriorate as the iron mordant in the madder brown oxidizes over time. Fabric historian Florence Montgomery dated "dark or shady patterns" to 1790; she occasionally called this color "plum," but it seems more a dark, chocolate brown rather than a purple. Montgomery described the tan grounds that date after 1800 as "Tan blotch . . . a rather smeary or uneven tan background color." The name "tea grounds" to describe a creamy tan, is a bit confusing until we remember that the English like their tea with milk. Madder dyes also produced the dark, "sad" red grounds.[4]

Bright blue grounds were quite popular, printed with Prussian blue or a complicated indigo discharge technique. The printer could dye grounds green by printing yellow atop blue. Montgomery called these overprinted grounds a "dipped green ground," a style most popular in the 1810s. The most unusual blotch ground is bright yellow, which looks like chrome yellow but might be quercitron, another fast, bright yellow dye.

Blotch-ground chintzes do not seem to have been printed with added grounds of purple, pink, bright red, or orange, colors that could have been printed with different techniques. And a true black ground was not used, since black was so hard to obtain in cotton until after 1890.

Reproduction quilt, *Stars in the Crown* by Karla Menaugh and designers at United Notions, 2001, Lawrence, Kansas, and Dallas, Texas, 67" x 67". Karla and I were inspired by early quilts featuring simple stars set on point with dark edge triangles. Because we were using strike-offs, we had only small swatches of fabric for the stars, so we were forced to think like the quiltmakers who worked during the decades when a yard of fabric cost a week's wages. The center echoes those quiltmakers' use of asymmetry and variable contrast. We sent the top off to United Notions, where they added borders of the Moda collection fabric called *Victoria's Crown*. As so often in art by committee, communications were problematic. We had no idea they'd add the two small inner borders of high contrast strips. Our idea for a soft-focus chintz quilt was updated and pulled together in modern fashion with their simple addition.

Roller Printing

Antique quilt, star medallion, 1825–1850, possibly Jacksonville, Illinois, 88" x 93". Collection of Kern and Barbara Jackson. Quilters in the first half of the century loved to combine small calicoes with larger-scale fabrics. Fabrics in the stars are primarily roller prints. The monochrome border print may be a woodblock chintz. Measure the repeat by estimating distance from the tip of one feather to the tip of another on a 93" side border. It's about 11½", a typical woodblock measurement; but roller prints ranged from about 12" to 15", so it's difficult to determine the technology.

" *Tell Susan to ask Mrs Booth for a quilt pattern called Tangle Britches which she has peised (sic) with pale blue calico.* "

LETTER FROM JAMES H. SMITH[5]

Stereograph, a management team inspecting a strike-off of roller-printed cotton, about 1900. The reverse of the photo noted that the Lawrence Mills in Massachusetts printed five million yards per week, enough to "reach around the world six times."

Stereograph of an "old lady" frightened by a cat fight, about 1870. To emphasize her age, she wears the mob cap fashionable generations earlier. The bed, a "French bed," is also old-fashioned, a style popular in the early nineteenth century. French beds were hung with less drapery than the older four-poster beds. Such open beds showed off patchwork quilts to better advantage. The bed quilt features sashing of large stripes, possibly 1820–1860.

As printing technology grew more sophisticated, the look of fabric changed. Among the important advancements in the 1790s was a new method for printing with cylinders or rollers. Scotsman Thomas Bell's method of mechanizing copper-plate printing eventually eliminated older techniques of plate and block printing. During the first half of the nineteenth century, however, the three printing methods co-existed while mills and nations competed to produce elegant, well-registered cottons in a wide range of colors at inexpensive prices. Printers combined techniques, for example, block printing over roller-printed grounds. They worked out ways to mechanize wooden blocks by attaching them to rollers. And, as always, there was the human hand. Unskilled laborers "penciled" details with brushes.

The rotary press or cylinder printing method was far more efficient than either block printing or plate printing. One could obtain the toile's detailed line drawing and the block print's color variety at a fast rate of production. Roller prints, however, had limitations. One was the reduced repeat. Copper-plates

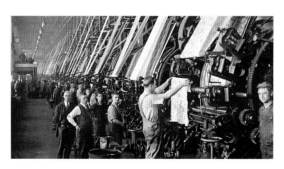

measured a yard or so long and prints were designed to fill the space. A roller was about half the size, with a fifteen-inch surface wrapped around the cylinder. Rollers, while effective in printing continuous pattern, did not lend themselves to the look of scenic toiles or grand botanicals.

The small repeat that rollers print so well became the standard look for inexpensive cottons. Rollers with incised lines did not easily produce large areas of color like blotch woodblock prints. New kinds of backgrounds developed to fill the areas between the figures.

Fancy Machine Grounds

The soft copper roller surfaces wore out quickly, requiring artists to re-engrave the designs. In 1808, Englishman Jacob Perkins realized that he could engrave steel plates (mills) and press them into the soft copper roller. When the copper surface wore away, mechanics merely stamped the copper roller again with the same steel master.

Joseph Lockett hired artists to engrave patterns for steel mills and sold the machined mills to other printers, who pressed background designs into their copper rollers. Lockett reportedly sold 20,000 different engraved patterns, such as fine lines and dots, honeycombs, seaweeds, lace, scrolls, and serpentine stripes. The old-fashioned name for backgrounds printed with these linear and dotted patterns is "fancy machine grounds."[7]

Amanda Thomas in Boonville, Missouri, with a baby quilt I made her in 1981. I found a terrific print with a fancy machine ground to feature between the stars, a thrill when reproduction fabrics with textured grounds were rare.

Reproduction quilt, *Feathered Fancy* by Roseanne Smith, 2003, Lawrence, Kansas, 88" x 88". Roseanne's interpretation of a classic early nineteeth-century pattern makes good use of a palette of primary colors.

Antique fabric from the heyday of the fancy machine ground, 1810-1840. Ground designs include dots, known as picotage, and all manner of squiggles.

Reproduction imitating the textures, picotage, and floral and geometric patterns found in the old, fancy machine grounds. The purple at the top right is a moiré, a printed imitation of the embossed silk known as watered silk because of its resemblance to ripples in a stream.

Stripes

Left: Tintype, about 1860. Wide stripes for women's clothing were in vogue in the 1840s and 1850s. Middle: Cased tintype, about 1860. Right: Cased tintype, about 1860. Box pleats and striped fabrics were the last word in fashion.

Technology changed fabric's appearance but taste also influenced production. Stripes were all the rage for clothing and furnishings on both sides of the Atlantic between 1790 and 1840. The up-to-date draped their four-poster beds, papered their walls, and covered their chairs with stripes. The look of a wide stripe was so important that women deprived of imported fabric for bed coverings pieced their own by cutting American calicoes into lengths and stitching them as stripes. The fad for striped furnishing fabrics encouraged quilters to set their blocks in long strips.

To fabric designers, stripes are a way to set figures. Striped sets can be hard-edged geometric lines or undulating paths of flowers or paisleys.

Designers also used stripes as backgrounds. Just like fancy machine grounds, striped grounds effectively used roller printing to fill large spaces. Background stripes might be wide, or narrow, and printed in pattern, line, or color. At the height of the craze for striped grounds, background stripes might show right through the figure. Floral figures were often com-

pletely unrelated to the striped ground. Florence Montgomery saw striped-ground fabric as poor taste. She described a particular print as an "unfortunate mixture of merely pretty, naturalistic flowers on a ground imitating a woven striped silk [that marked] a low point in chintz design."[8]

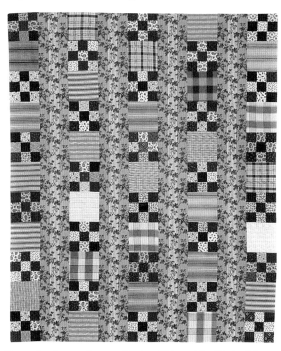

Reproduction quilt top, *Road to Richmond* by Karla Menaugh, 2003, Lawrence, Kansas, 54" x 66". A reproduction quilt much in the spirit of the antique, which is at top right on page 31.

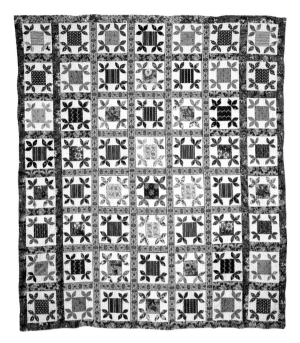

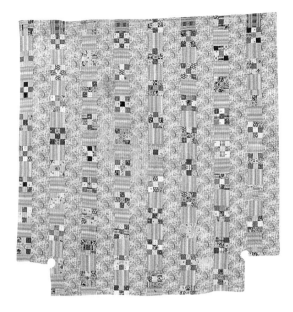

Each to her own taste. Fashionable women of the 1850s thought the print under discussion the pinnacle of good design. They loved a bold mix of pattern, of large florals shot through with colorful, geometric stripes. Like other busy, large-scale prints, complex striped grounds fell out of fashion by the time of the Civil War.

TOP LEFT
Antique quilt top, Turkey Tracks or Honeybee variation, found in Maine, estimated date 1830–1850. Collection of Terry Clothier Thompson.

TOP RIGHT
Antique quilt, *Nine Patch*, estimated date 1830–1860. Characteristics such as the strip set, the soft contrast, and many scraps of the block, plate, and roller prints mark this quilt as dating to the years before the Civil War.

LOWER LEFT
Reproduction quilt, *Turkey Red, Turkey Blue* by Georgann Eglinski, 2002, Lawrence, Kansas, 85" x 88". Machine quilted by Lori Kukuk. Reproduction quilts often grow out of the perfect piece of fabric. Georgann found a stripe alternating wild turkeys with a bright blue floral, designed by Kaye England for South Sea Imports. She pieced in many more stripes using Turkey red and chrome orange prints, a serpentine stripe, and a bias-printed plaid that reads like a stripe for the border.

THE REPUBLIC OF TEXAS

JANUARY 24, 1843

"[Send me] furniture calico, but take care to select none such, as will exhibit Turkey Gobblers, Peacocks, Bears, Elephants, wild Boars or Stud Horses!!! Vines, Flowers, or any figure of taste; you can select. "

LETTER FROM PRESIDENT SAM HOUSTON TO HIS AGENT IN NEW ORLEANS[9]

Thinking in Strips

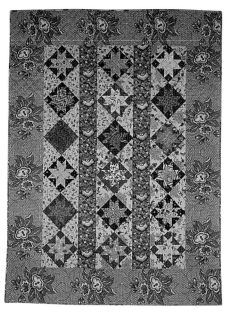

Block Size	Strip Width (finished)	Cut Squares for Setting Triangles (Cut in quarters diagonally)	Cut Squares for Corner Triangles (Cut in half diagonally)
4"	5⅝"	7"	3¾"
5"	7⅛"	8⅜"	4½"
6"	8½"	9¾"	5⅛"
7"	9⅞"	11¼"	5⅞"
8"	11⅜"	12⅝"	6⅝"
9"	12¾"	14"	7¼"
10"	14⅛"	15½"	8"
11"	15½"	16⅞"	8¾"
12"	17"	18¼"	9⅜"

*Reproduction Quilt, *Strippy Stars* by Jo Morton, 1999, Nebraska City, Nebraska, 43" x 57". Quilted by Stella Schaffert. Photograph by Mark Jewell. Great chintz plus a strip set, a simple formula for an authentic-looking reproduction.

Strip quilts look old-fashioned because American quilters generally abandoned the strip set about the time of the Civil War (exceptions include Flying Geese and Amish and Mennonite sets). If you want reproduction quilts to look like survivors from the early nineteenth century, think in strips. You can set any simple block into a strip set. The rules and the math are simple.

• **Grain line.** Piece blocks so edges are on grain. You'll be piecing the straight edge of the block to the bias edge of the setting triangles.

• **Strip Width.** Use the chart to calculate strip width if you know block size.

• **Setting Triangles.** The diagonal measurement of the block is the length of the long leg of the setting triangle. For example, an 8" block is 11⅜" diagonally, which is the measurement for the long leg of the triangle. You will need to add seams. See the chart for measurements to rotary cut setting triangles. This will put the outside edge of the setting triangle along the straight grain of the fabric.

• **Corner Triangles.** You'll need 4 for each strip. You can cut these oversized if you wish and trim later.

• **Balance.** When planning a strip quilt, use an odd number of strips and place unpieced strips along the edges.

• **Borders.** In the old days they usually left the top and bottom unbordered. If you do use a top and bottom border, don't miter your border corners. The strips go right across the ends and it looks more authentic.

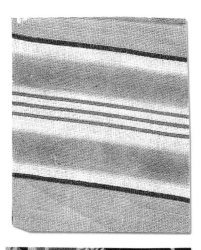

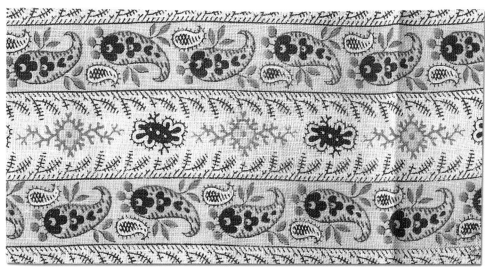

Antique fabric, stripe sets, and stripe grounds, 1820–1850. Designers fit an amazing amount of pattern into one print. The pink in the center has a figure of brown *mignonettes* (little fancy) atop a pink-and-white fancy machine ground, plus an eccentric brown and white stripe, a ground that dominates the print.

Reproduction fabric, stripe sets, and stripe grounds. The madder orange stripe above imitates a Centennial print (1876). The others mimic prints from about 1810 to 1890.

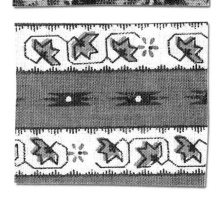

Pillar Prints

The early nineteenth-century mania for stripes found expression in pillar prints that echo the Classical architecture of ancient Greece and Rome. Stripes take the form of fluted, rounded columns interrupted by ornate capitals and garlands of flowers. These large-scale "architectural prints" were printed in England. The French, the Dutch, and the Swiss had no interest in printing or using them and, indeed, the biggest market seems to have been America during the decades when Classical style influenced everything from the lines of women's dress to the colonnades of Southern mansions. Americans styling their new nation on the ideals of ancient Greece were infatuated with all forms of Classical design.

Pillar prints draped windows and beds and were layered in whole-cloth quilts between 1800 and 1860. Perfect for borders and especially for the setting strips in strip quilts, pillar prints were also pieced into patchwork. By 1840, the fabric was behind the times for interiors, but quilters for decades continued to salvage patches from their old drapes. Pillar prints are found in quilts right up to the Civil War.

The original pillar prints were printed with woodblocks. By about 1825, fabric mills printed line detail in columns and flowers with copper rollers, and added more color in leaves and backgrounds with woodblocks. Many pillar prints feature popular early nineteenth-century blotch grounds.

Reproduction quilt, *R. Porter's Star* by Bobbi Finley, 2001, San Jose, California, 78" x 85". Machine quilted by Pamela Uhlig. Bobbi's inspiration was a quilt signed and dated in the 1770s, belonging to the American Museum in Bath, England. The original predated pillar prints, but Bobbi's intent was to interpret a look rather than make a close copy. The lesson to be learned from the past is in her skillful use of close contrast.[10]

Reproduction quilt, *Box Pattern* by Georgann Eglinski, 2002, Lawrence, Kansas, 87" x 87". Quilted by Rosie Mayhew.

The pattern we generally call Baby's Blocks has over a dozen published names. An 1882 needlework book called it Block Pattern or Box Pattern. Variegated Diamonds and Shifting Cubes are other names from the turn of the last century. Georgann picked up the color scheme for the 60° diamonds from the pillar print, a combination of bright Prussian blue, sad madder red, and yellow-green on a greenish-yellow ground that looks to be a copy of an oak dye called quercitron. Mitered border strips are found in nineteenth-century quilts, but they are rather uncommon.

Antique fabric, pillar print with blue blotch ground, 1800–1830. Rollers probably printed madder red lines defining the figure, woodblocks the other shades— blue and possibly a yellow that has faded quite a bit.

Serpentine Stripes and Eccentrics

LEFT
Carte de visite, "Sister Ellen," Washington, Missouri, about 1865. The cut of Ellen's dress and her wide belt seem chic for Civil War-era Missouri, but the fabric of serpentine stripe seems a bit dated. Like many other women during the War, Ellen, deprived of yard goods, might have ripped out an old dress to fashion a new one.

RIGHT
Cased tintype, woman in a dress of eccentric print, about 1860. Old-fashioned head wear and a Bible indicate a conservative woman, quite a contrast to the eccentric print that looks so modern to our eyes.

ESTATE INVENTORY OF ANNE SHEDDEN,
PENNSYLVANIA, SEPTEMBER 24, 1829

1 white bed quilt with fringe $6.00
1 other quilt calico (sic) patchwork $2.50
1 other quilt $1.75
1 other quilt $2.25
2 other quilts $3.00
1 other quilt $1.62
3 bed quilts woolen $6.00[11]

Like their reptilian namesake, serpentine stripes wiggle across the surface. Their meandering lines of pattern, either floral or geometric, softened the hard edges of conventional stripes to flatter the early Victorian figure. Serpentine stripes were quite popular for clothing and quilts from about 1830 through the Civil War.

"Eccentrics," a subcategory of serpentine stripes, were geometric fine lines with jagged or wavy distortions. The print style was invented, according to textile historian Florence Pettit, when a pinstripe crimped in the roller. Rather than discarding the misprint, the enterprising millowner, Mr. Lane, created a new fad. The accidental pattern became

known as "Lane's Net," and was so popular that mills printed yardage enough for 100,000 dresses, according to one account keeper of the era. Designers find inspiration everywhere, so it may be that an English printer of the 1820s saw possibilities in misprints of the new roller presses, but Lane's Net is far too regular to have been created by accident. Whatever his inspiration, Mr. Lane was savvy enough to create a fashion that lasted for a generation.[12]

Antique quilt (detail) in a star design, pieced of a variety of eccentric stripes, found in Missouri. Estimated date 1840–1860. Indigo prints usually had white figures; a popular exception featured bright yellow figures, a striking color combination that added to the eccentric look.

Shopping List for Fabric of the Rising Sun

- ◆ Chintzes with colored blotch grounds
- ◆ Chintzes with fancy machine grounds
- ◆ Stripe Sets, wide and narrow
- ◆ Stripe Grounds
- ◆ Pillar Prints
- ◆ Serpentine Stripes
- ◆ Eccentric Prints

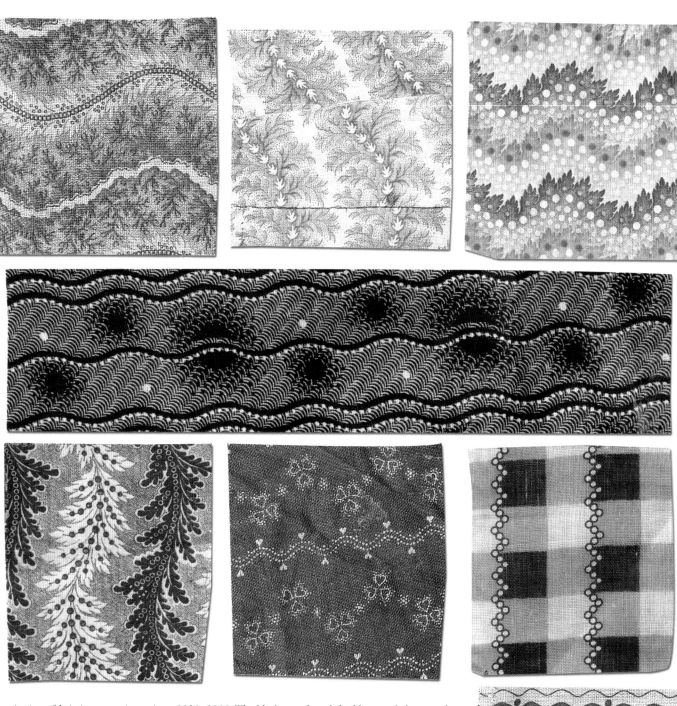

Antique fabric in serpentine stripes, 1820–1900. The black swatch and the blue one below are the newest pieces, dating to 1900, the product of a revival of interest in serpentine stripes and eccentrics in new shades and dyes.

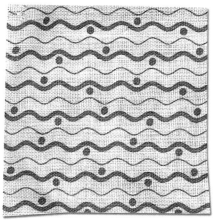

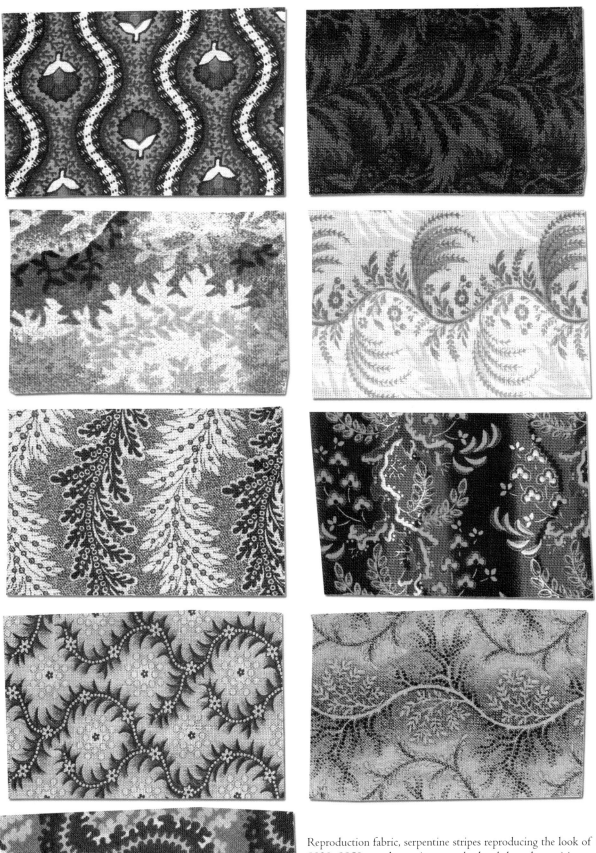

Reproduction fabric, serpentine stripes reproducing the look of the 1820–1850 era when stripes were both subtle and surprising.

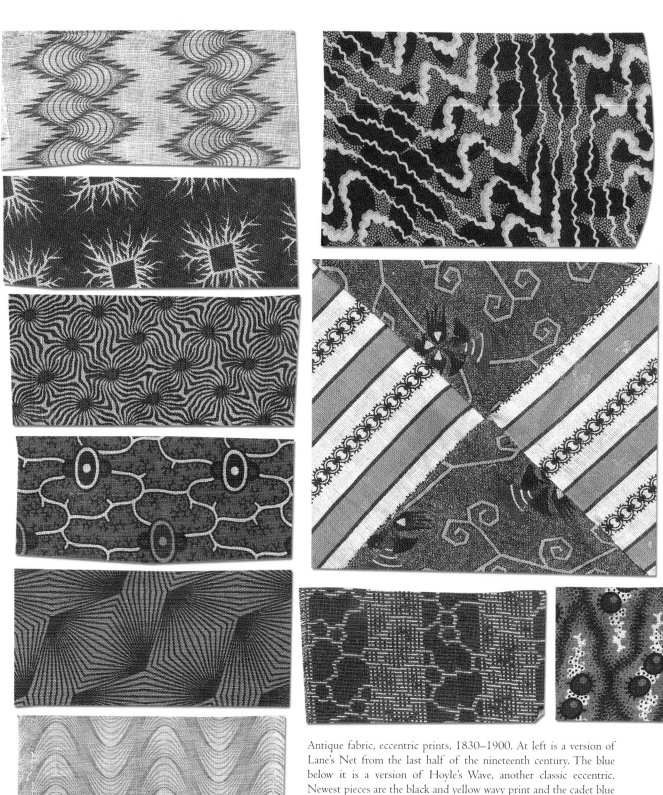

Antique fabric, eccentric prints, 1830–1900. At left is a version of Lane's Net from the last half of the nineteenth century. The blue below it is a version of Hoyle's Wave, another classic eccentric. Newest pieces are the black and yellow wavy print and the cadet blue with semetric designs, both from about 1900.

Reproduction fabric, eccentrics in squiggles, crackles, and jagged lines, including a copy of Lane's Net in red and several versions of Hoyle's Wave.

Rising Sun

Reproduction quilt, *Rising Sun* by Carol Gilham Jones, 2002, Lawrence, Kansas, 56" x 56". Machine quilted by Pamela Mayfield.

Carol's inspiration, pieced about 1840, was pictured in the Smithsonian Institution's catalog Calico and Chintz. *In the original full-sized quilt, sunbursts rise in alternating dark and light blocks, a rather sophisticated design idea called counterchange. Carol pieced the sunbursts over paper foundations, using reproduction prints recalling the 1800–1840 era.*[13]

FINISHED QUILT, 56" X 56" **BLOCK, 14" X 14" FINISHED** **BORDER, 7" FINISHED**

FABRIC REQUIREMENTS

Light botanical print: 1 yard for 5 blocks

Dark botanical print: 1⅓ yards for border

Dark calico: 1 yard for 4 blocks and smaller corner blocks

Selection of rainbow prints, serpentine stripes, sprigs, eccentrics, and floral trails: ¼ yard each of 9 light and 9 dark fabrics for the suns (fat quarters are fine)

Backing: 3½ yards

Batting: 60" x 60"

Binding: ½ yard

CUTTING

•Cut 4 strips 7½" x 42½" from the dark botanical print for the border.

•Use pattern (A) to cut 20 pieces from the light botanical print (4 per block) and 16 pieces from the dark calico. Set these aside to sew conventionally to the paper-pieced suns.

•Use pattern (B) to cut 16 pieces from the dark calico for the corner blocks (4 per block). Set these aside to sew conventionally to the paper-pieced suns.

•Use pattern (C) to cut 13 circles for the center of the suns to match the fabric in each block.

THE QUILT TOP

Piecing Over Paper Foundations

1. Paper piece the suns by machine. You can't paper piece a diamond shape using the foundation method, so Carol created the illusion of diamonds by paper piecing 2 rings of triangles in matching fabric. Each ring is made up of 4 arcs—4 quarter circles. The smaller, inner arc forms the center of the 9 large blocks and the 4 smaller suns in the corner blocks. The larger arc forms the outer ring in the 9 large blocks. (Foundation patterns are on page 45.)

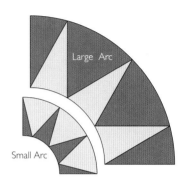

2. Make 52 photocopies or tracings of the small arc (3½") and 36 of the large arc (7").

3. Use the small arc to piece the 13 small suns, as shown. Match the colors in groups of 4. Do not remove the paper.

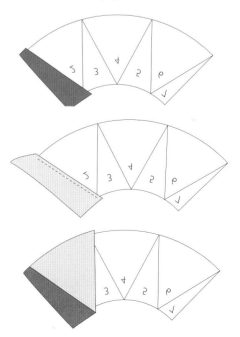

4. Sew 4 arcs into a small sun.

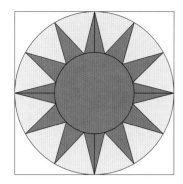

5. Add the center (C). You may piece or appliqué the circle on top. Make 4 small suns.

6. Sew the 4 small suns into corner blocks by adding 4 pieces (B). Remove the paper foundation.

7. Use the large foundations to piece the large arcs in the same manner. Again, match the colors in groups of 4, but also match the colors to the smaller arcs so you will have matching sunbursts. Piece 36 larger arcs in groups of 4. Do not remove the paper.

8. Sew the matching inner and outer arcs together.

9. Sew 4 arcs into a large sun.

10. Add the center (C). You may piece or appliqué the circle on top. Make 9 large suns.

11. Sew the large suns into squares by adding piece (A). Remove the paper foundation.

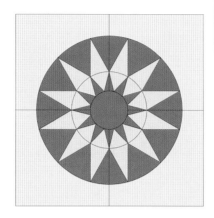

Setting

1. Sew 3 rows of 3 blocks each, alternating dark and light backgrounds. Press.

2. Join the rows. Press.

Border

1. Add the top and bottom borders to the quilt top.

2. Piece the small sun blocks to the ends of the side borders, checking border length to fit quilt top.

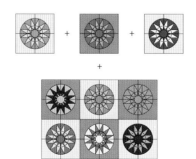

3. Add the side borders.

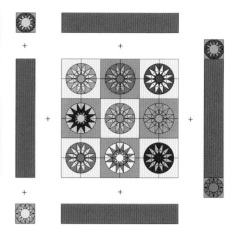

QUILTING

1. Layer and baste (page 125).

2. Quilt by hand or machine. Pamela Mayfield machine quilted a grid of 2½" diagonal lines across the patchwork, a typical utilitarian quilting style in the nineteenth century. She quilted a line of spirals in the border. In each corner block she outline quilted the sun's rays in lines about ¼" apart.

3. Bind the quilt (page 126).

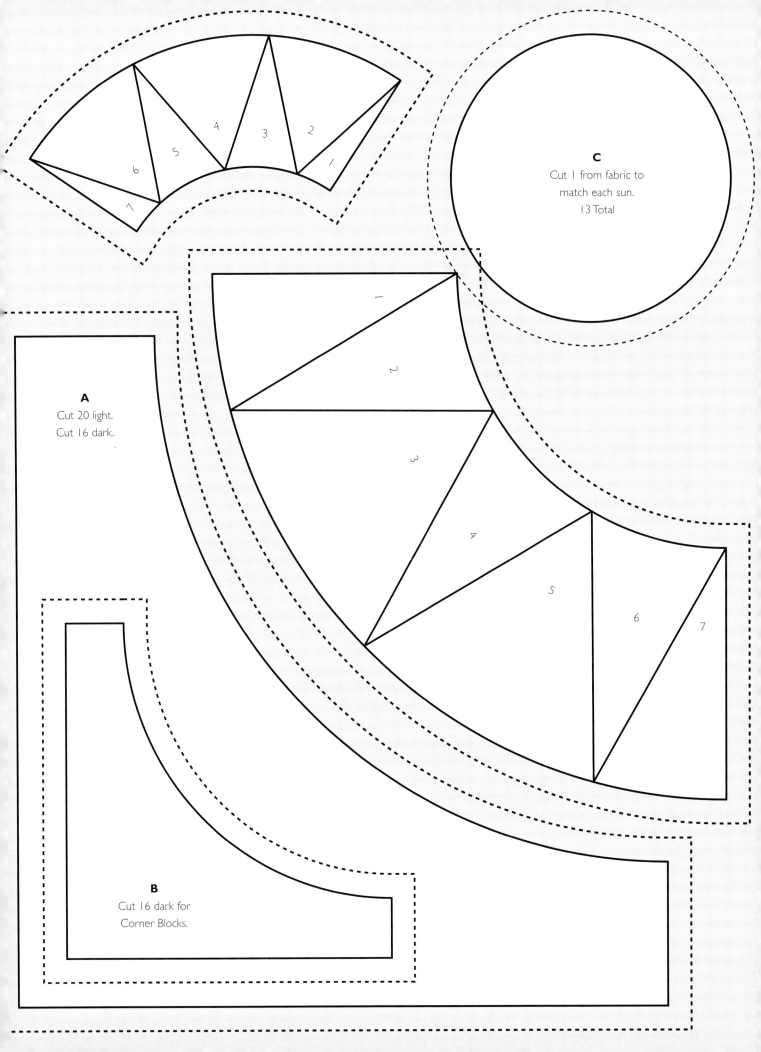

4
5
3
6
2
7
1

C
Cut 1 from fabric to
match each sun.
13 Total

1
2
3
4
5
6
7

A
Cut 20 light.
Cut 16 dark.

B
Cut 16 dark for
Corner Blocks.

Ocean Waves

or Tents of Armageddon

Reproduction quilt, *Ocean Waves* by Barbara Brackman, 2002, Lawrence, Kansas, 42" x 51". Machine quilted by Rosie Mayhew.

I made a close copy of a little quilt I own that looks to have been pieced from a scrapbag of chintzes and calicoes from a wide range of dates—1820 to 1860. The back of the original is a toile, which may date to 1790. (See page 5 for a detail.) The quilter cleverly framed the design with dark brown triangles, many of which are now worn due to oxidization of the iron mordant. The quilt was probably finished after 1850, as a few of the paisleys look to date from after the Civil War, and the machine chain-stitch in the binding is 1850s or later. Yet much fabric is earlier, as are design ideas, such as blocks on point, dark edge triangles, and the chintz border.

Did the allover pattern of triangles have a traditional name in the mid-nineteenth century? We have no records, but the Ladies' Art Company catalog called it Ocean Waves at the end of the century. The Spencer Museum of Art at the University of Kansas owns a version that has been called Tents of Armageddon in their catalogs for years. I've looked through their accession files on the quilt but found no information about the source for that dramatic name.

FINISHED QUILT, 42" X 50½"   BLOCKS, 3" X 3" FINISHED   BORDER, 4" FINISHED

Antique quilt, *Ocean Waves*, estimated date 1850–1870.

FABRIC REQUIREMENTS

A great quilt for using all your reproduction prints! If you are buying fabric, buy quarter yards (long or fat) except for the border.

Very dark prints: ¼ yard each of 4 fabrics for the edge triangles
Light prints: ¼ yard each of 10–12 fabrics
Medium to dark prints: ¼ yard each of 10–12 fabrics
Botanical chintz: 1½ yards for the border
Backing: 2⅝ yards
Batting: 46" x 55"
Binding: See discussion at end of project, or purchase ½ yard white fabric.

CUTTING

Sort the very dark fabrics for edge triangles. You will need 32 quarter-square triangles for the sides, top, and bottom, and 4 half-square triangles for the corners.

+ Cut 16 very dark squares 5½" x 5½". Cut it in quarters diagonally for the corners.

+ Cut 1 very dark square 3" x 3" Cut each in half diagonally.

+ Cut 72 light squares 3⅞" x 3⅞". Cut each in half diagonally.

+ Cut 72 medium to dark squares 3⅞" x 3⅞". Cut each in half diagonally.

+ Cut 2 strips 4½" x 42½" for the top and bottom borders.

+ For the border, cut 2 strips 4½" x 47" from the botanical chintz for the sides.

NOTE: Although the quilt is sewn together on the straight of the grain, it hangs on the bias. This may pull the top out of square if the project is delayed during construction. I have allowed extra length in cutting the borders "just in case."

THE QUILT TOP

Blocks

1. Sew 1 light triangle and 1 medium to dark triangle to make a block. You want a very scrappy look, so try not to duplicate the blocks. Make 143

blocks. There will be 2 extra.

2. Sew the blocks into strips. You'll be piecing straight strips, but they are sewn together diagonally. You will need 2 rows each of 1, 3, 5, 7, 9, 11, and 13 blocks; and 3 rows each of 15 blocks, for a total of 17 rows. The darker fabric should always be "up" when you sew the blocks into rows.

3. Sew 2 dark edge triangles to the end of each row **except** for 2 of the rows containing 15 blocks.

4. Decide which of the 2 remaining 15-block rows will be above the middle 15-block row and which will be below. Keep the dark fabrics "up." Sew an edge triangle to one end and a corner triangle to the opposite end of each row.

5. Sew the strips together in diagonal rows.

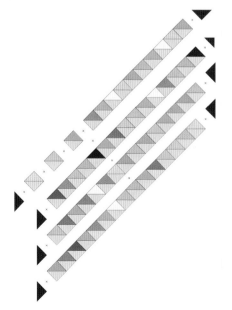

Borders

1. Referring to Butted Borders (page 125), measure quilt and trim side border strips.

2. Add the side borders. Press.

3. Repeat Step 1 and trim top and bottom border strips.

4. Add the top and bottom borders. Press.

QUILTING

1. Layer and baste (page 125).

2. Rosie Mayhew machine quilted a traditional utilitarian design that Rose Kretsinger called "Hanging Diamonds" in *The Romance of the Patchwork Quilt in America*.[14] Rosie quilted vertical lines by quilting through the points of the triangles, parallel to the sides of the quilt top. She then stitched a diagonal line through the middle of each row of blocks.

She quilted a feather in the border.

BINDING

The original quilt is bound with white cotton twill tape about ¾" wide, never a really popular finish but a good period look.

You may be able to find something similar. The original quilt-maker didn't turn the edges under; she finished off the binding on the front with a machine stitch from a chain-stitch machine. I used striped twill tape that Moda ties around their fat quarter packs. (I had to do a little begging among friends.) See Binding on page 126.

[1] Allie Bayne Windham Webb, *Mistress of Evergreen Plantation: Rachel O'Connor's Legacy of Letters* (Albany: State University of New York, 1983) Pg. 167.

[2] Melvin Thomas Copeland, *The Cotton Manufacturing Industry of the United States* (New York: Augustus Kelley, 1966).

[3] United States Census. XVIII.

[4] Florence Montgomery, *Printed Textiles: English and American Cottons and Linens 1750-1850* (New York: Viking Press, 1970) Pg. 325.

[5] Letter from James H. Smith, Manuscript Collection, Illinois State Historical Society.

[6] Robert Bishop and Patricia Coblentz, *New Discoveries in American Quilts* (New York: E.P. Dutton & Co., 1975) Plate 12.

[7] Adamson, Pp. 28-29. Montgomery, Pg. 307.

[8] Montgomery, Pg. 309.

[9] Letter quoted in James L. Haley, *Sam Houston* (Norman: University of Oklahoma, 2002) Pg. 265.

[10] Sheila Betterton, *Quilts and Coverlets from the American Museum in Britain* (Bath, England: American Museum, 1978) Pg. 51.

[11] Jeannette Lasansky, *Pieced By Mother* (Lewisburg, PA: Oral Traditions Project, 1988) Pg. 27.

[12] Florence Pettit, *America's Printed and Painted Fabrics 1600-1900* (New York: Hastings House, 1970) Pp. 212, 231.

[13] Adamson, Pg. 41.

[14] Carrie A. Hall and Rose G. Kretsinger, *Romance of the Patchwork Quilt in America* (Caldwell, ID: Caxton Printers, 1935) Pg. 271.

An old silk bonnet passed down in a Quaker family with the accouterments of a typical young American woman in about 1860. Among the sewing tools is a flag sewing box, possibly dating to the Civil War. It was red, white, and blue before the blue field bled into the red and white striped silk. The small brass stencil near the center was used to ink one's name on calling cards or album quilt blocks. The antique quilt top in the Railroad Crossing pattern is pieced from a scrapbag of popular dress prints in Prussian blues, double pinks, madder-style browns, and purples.

CHAPTER 3

The Fabric of Young America
1840-1865

LOWELL, MASSACHUSETTS, ABOUT 1840

" *[Emilie] was always thinking what she could do for others . . . she gave money to send to the missionaries, or to help build new churches in the city, when she was earning only eight or ten dollars a month clear of her board, and could afford herself but one 'best dress' besides her working clothes. That best dress was often nothing but a Merrimack print.* "

LUCY LARCOM RECALLING HER SISTER, A MILL GIRL[1]

Cased tintype, girl in a printed plaid dress, about 1860. Girls as young as eleven, Lucy Larcom's age when she entered the mill, worked in the spinning and weaving rooms. Printing the cloth was men's work.

Lucy and Emilie Larcom grew to adulthood in Massachusetts as members of a generation who called themselves Young America. Born citizens of a democracy, rather than subjects of a king, they possessed a remarkable sense of independence, differing in many ways from their parents who had lived through the break with England. Women of the Larcom sisters' generation were the first to work in factories. Paid a bit more than they required for room and board, mill girls had extra money to give to missions, save for marriage, or spend on clothing. They were among the best customers for the cotton calicoes they spun and wove.

North and South expressed the independent spirit in diverging paths as the two regions viewed themselves as contrasting cultures with competing goals. The agricultural South looked more and more to cotton for its wealth, relying on slave labor despite emancipation throughout Europe and its colonies. An increasingly urban North banked on industry.

Chief among their factory goods was cotton cloth. The contentious but efficient team of Southern cotton plantations and Northern textile mills continued to drive down the price of cotton cloth. Emilie Larcom, earning about $3 a week, might pay twenty cents a yard for calico from the Merrimack mill. America still relied on Europe for the best chintzes, silks, and wools, but grew independent in the production of inexpensive cottons—the calicoes and ginghams of every-day clothing.

Mrs. Columbia tries to patch the Union, 1860 cartoon from *Vanity Fair.*

Antique quilt, stars in a zigzag or fence rail set, estimated date, 1840–1860. The fence rail set was popular at the end of the century. However, everything else about the quilt from fabric to backing looks consistent with a mid-century date. Everyday patchwork combined a variety of cotton plains and prints—*foulards*, stripes, printed plaids, and generic calicoes—arranged in combinations that appear a bit haphazard to our eyes. Some blocks show high contrast, others low—by art or accident. Star points, possibly once Prussian blue solids, have faded to pale tan.

A hoop skirt manufacturing company, *Harper's Weekly*, February 1859

" WOODSTOCK, VERMONT
SEPTEMBER 13, 1845
Dear Father,
I want you to consent to let me go to Lowell if you can. I think it would be much better for me than to stay about here. I could earn more to begin with than I can any where about here. I am in need of clothes which I cannot get if I stay about here. "

LETTER FROM MARY PAUL, WHO HOPED TO WORK IN A TEXTILE FACTORY[2]

Quiltmakers could now afford to sort scraps by fiber, weight, and style, making quilts exclusively of silk or wool and, especially cotton.

The 25-year span between 1840 and the end of the Civil War was a golden age in America's quiltmaking. Superb handwork reflected the last glory of hand sewing before the sewing machine's arrival. Design explored new pattern and style, while different cultures, such as the Pennsylvania Germans, added ideas to the look of the patchwork quilt. And women all over the country had access to imported and domestic cottons that were both inexpensive and intricately printed.

"Godey's Unrivaled Colored Fashions," from *Godey's Lady's Book* in 1854. Elaborate evening costumes featured an off-the-shoulder look and wide skirts. The silks may have been imported but the underpinnings were domestic.

LEFT

Stereograph, about 1865. The coach driver insists that the traveler store hoops atop the coach, giving viewers a rather risqué peek at underwear. "Werry sorry Mam, but leave yer Krinerline outside."

RIGHT

Carte de visite, Bloomsburg, Pennsylvania, about 1865. In a day dress typical of 1855 to 1865, voluminous skirts (probably made of combination wool fabric) are propped over a frame of hoops. Sleeves wide at the elbow and hair parted in the middle added to the desirable horizontal look, punctuated by a tiny corseted waist wrapped in a wide belt.

LEFT

Women's street wear was usually made of silk, wool, or the combination fabrics delaine (wool/cotton) or challis (wool/silk), which could be printed like the fabric in the Log Cabin quilt, made about 1870. The dress, a little earlier, is a wool/silk combination called "changeable" in which the fabric changes color as warps and wefts reflect different light.

RIGHT

*Reproduction quilt, Adam and Eve by Shauna Oak Christensen, 2000, Lawrence, Kansas, 84" x 84". Hand quilted by Anne Thomas. Inspired by several antique quilts featuring the tale of the Garden of Eden, Shauna appliquéd Eve in her pink birthday suit with a hoop-skirted silhouette. The original designer couldn't imagine true nudity, even in Paradise.

Prussian Blue

Reproduction quilt, *John Brown's Bedquilt*, designed by Barbara Brackman, pieced by Shirlene Wedd and friends, 2000, Lawrence, Kansas, 91" x 105". Machine quilted by Rosie Mayhew. The Kansas State Historical Society commissioned a period piece for a cabin in Osawatomie, where famed abolitionist John Brown visited his sister Florella Adair. Inspired by a quilt made in 1843 in Wayne County, Ohio,[3] we designed a quilt Florella might have brought from Ohio when she came to Kansas in 1854. The blocks on point are pieced from soft double pinks, lots of browns, and Prussian blues framed by a pillar print she might have cut from her old drapes.

Technological strides are quite apparent in mid-century quilts. Increasingly sophisticated chemists discovered new forms of natural dyes for which raw materials were mined rather than cultivated. Prussian blue is a mineral dye that colors cotton a variety of shades, the most distinctive being a bright royal blue. Unlike indigo, which works most efficiently as a background color, Prussian blue can be the figure in a print as well as the ground.

Prussian blue, (the name applies to both color and dye) was popular for dyeing blue wool uniforms, a use reflected in other military names such as Lafayette blue and Napoleon's blue. The color, also used for pigments and paint, is familiar to children who grew up with crayons labeled Prussian Blue before 1958 when the name changed to Midnight Blue. During the last half of the nineteenth century, America's greenback dollars obtained their color from a combination of Prussian blue and chrome yellow.

Dye historian James Liles told the story of German chemists who discovered Prussian blue in 1788. Seeking shelter from the rain in a blacksmith's shop, they found a blue puddle. They calculated that the color resulted from a mix of ashes, rust, and rain water. Rust was from iron horseshoes; ashes from the forge that contained charcoal and bits of the horses' hooves. The happy accident produced a pool of iridescent blue that would permanently dye wool, silk, or cotton. Like most stories of discovery, this one is probably more myth than fact, but it's a good way to remember that Prussian blue has both mineral and animal components. In the nineteenth century, the animal component often came from scavengers who recycled old boots and shoes by selling them to mills for use in Prussian blue.[4]

Historian Rita Adrosko traces the first American Prussian blue dyeing to 1832, probably for wool. Scraps of Prussian blue cottons don't appear in quilts until the 1840s, many decades after the dye's discovery. Prussian blues were most popular for quilts and clothing here during the 1850s.[5]

The dye is fast to light and acid solutions, but a strong hot alkali solution, such as laundry soap, breaks down the blue, leaving a tan color. (See the quilt on page 52.) Solid blue cottons in nineteenth-century quilts are often streaked or faded. Continued laundering could completely eliminate the blue.

Most of the greens in nineteenth-century quilts were over-dyed in a combination of Prussian blue and chrome yellow. Laundering in an alkali solution could deteriorate the blue, leaving a distinctive yellow-green color. It seems that plain blues and green calicoes are especially susceptible to this alkali discharge, while bright Prussian blue prints of the era do not fade. Stripes, plaids, florals, and rainbow prints maintain a wonderful vibrancy despite washing. It may be that the steam printing process (see page 58) renders colors faster than simple dyeing.

A classic mid-century example of technology dictating taste is the Prussian blue and iron buff print, a bright blue with a rather dull tan. Chemistry allowed printers to easily combine two closely related dyes. Dye historian Martin Bide described Prussian blue as iron acetate with potassium ferricyanide. Iron buff is iron acetate with alkali to give iron oxide. The blue and buff combination was printed in what is called "raised style," in which one chemical is printed on the fabric and a second chemical then "raised" or developed the color. James Liles phrased it another way, classifying iron buff as a discharged version of Prussian blue. A strong alkali solution, the second chemical, removes or discharges the blue color, leaving the flat-colored tan. Printers made a virtue of blue's tendency to fade to tan by combining the two colors inexpensively. Blue and buff cottons were ultra smart for furnishings and women's clothing in the 1840s and 1850s. We also see them in quilts from about 1840 through 1865.[6]

After the Civil War, the bright blue typical of Prussian blue was no longer popular for clothing, yet the dye continued to produce other shades through the early twentieth century. It may be that the distinctive blue-violet shirtings of the 1870–1890 period were dyed with Prussian blue. I've seen several pieces of clothing in which that color is completely discharged in spots, indicating the alkali/laundry problem.

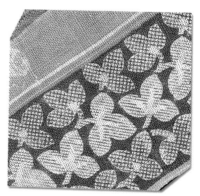

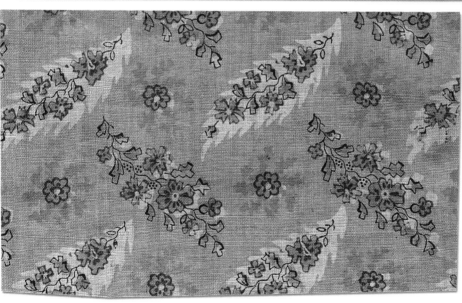

Antique fabric and a block in a wide variety of blues, most from the 1830–1860 period. The newest is the hard-edged stripe in blue-violet, a typical shirting from the 1870s. Prussian blue was often printed with browns ranging from buff to chocolate madders.

Reproduction fabric in shades echoing Prussian blues. Look for blues brighter than indigo's navy. Prussian blue, unlike most indigo prints, can be figure or ground. Popular in the 1800–1825 era for blotch grounds (above), the dye was used in the 1840s and 1850s for rainbow prints. Thirty years later, Prussian blue dyed neat shirtings (center left).

Rainbow Prints

Reproduction quilt, *Barbara Fritchie Star*, designed by Barbara Brackman, pieced by Shirlene Wedd, appliquéd by Jean Pearson Stanclift, hand quilted by Anne Thomas, 2000, Lawrence, Kansas, 90" x 90". In the early twentieth century, this pieced star came to be named for Civil War heroine Barbara Fritchie, who was made famous for standing up to Confederate invaders in a poem by John Greenleaf Whittier. We dug deep into my collection of Prussian blue and Turkey red reproductions to make this quilt with a patriotic border drawn from a quilt dated 1863. A few rainbow prints add depth to the design. The lesson from the past: "Pieced quilt—appliquéd border." Today we think in terms of piecing or appliqué, but many of the best antique quilts combine techniques.

Chintzes and calicoes grew increasingly intricate as chemists learned to obtain interesting effects by controlling the processes involved in printing fabric. Shaded stripes known as rainbow prints were first produced with woodblocks in the 1820s and became more common as printers perfected roller printing technology.

Rainbow prints are shaded from dark to light in regular waves. Variations include a rainbow of different colors or different intensities of a single color. Stripes might wash smoothly from one shade to the next or make the transition with ripples and zigzags. Shading affects either figure or ground, most often the ground, in mid-nineteenth-century fabrics.

Hazel Clark, writing in the British journal *Textile History*, noted that rainbow printing was dependent on the invention of "steam printing," which involved fixing color by wrapping cloth on perforated cylinders and steaming it for a half hour, then processing it with an alkaline solution of alum. Steaming was introduced to the printworks in Lancashire about 1813 and was, according to Lancashire printer Benjamin Hargreaves, "a great revolution in the trade."[7]

Historian Catherine Lynn dated the term "rainbow" to an 1826 reference to wallpapers, also printed in rainbow style. The earliest fabric reference she found was 1846. In 1850, Benjamin Hargreaves described "rainbow stripes, of steam pink, blue, green, and orange, afterwards crossed with paler shades of the same colours . . . the effect . . . brilliant in the extreme." Other names for the style are *fondu* prints, from the French word meaning to melt or dissolve, and *ombre*, French for shaded or tinted.[8]

Rainbow shading was exceptionally popular in varying intensities of bright blue cottons obtained with Prussian blue. Shaded grounds were fashionable behind stripes and in plaids, as well as under figures like florals and scrolls. Mid-nineteenth-century quiltmakers loved them for sets and borders, pieced designs, and appliqué. The skillful artists who made Baltimore Album quilts used shaded colors to suggest the dimension of baskets, watermelon rinds, and architectural columns in their pictorial appliqué.

Rainbow fabrics, which appear rather garish to our eyes, were considered surprisingly tasteful for American dresses between 1840 and 1860. Early photographs feature women clad in their best rainbow plaids and stripes. The prints fell out of fashion for clothing in the late 1850s, but continued popular in quilts until the end of the Civil War. During the 1880s and 1890s shaded prints enjoyed a revival, but later prints, no longer in buffs and bright blues, are just as likely to feature shaded figures as shaded grounds.

Ambrotype, woman in a rainbow print dress, about 1857.

Ohio, About 1850

" Money was scarce and the outlook rather forbidding ... Brother McConnell consoled my wife with the thought that probably she could afford to wear '6 cent calico' before the year ended. "

Minister Hugh Fisher recalling the first years of his marriage[9]

Antique fabric, rainbow or *ombre* prints, many dating between 1840 and 1860. Blues blurred to green or buff, purples to brown, and browns to tan. The oldest piece is probably a chintz from 1820 (lower center). Newer prints from 1880 to 1900 include the leaf at lower right, in which figure rather than ground changes shade. The red ground print at lower left dates to that same time.

Reproduction fabric capturing the rainbow fad of the 1840s and its revival about 1890. The brown leaf print (left) is a reduced version of the original.

Turkey Red

Carte de visite, Morris, Illinois, about 1870. Baby clothes, like the jacket with added trim, were often made of Turkey red cotton.

Turkey red dye takes its name from the old Turkish empire. The processes were invented in India, the heart of cotton traditions, and exported west to the Ottoman Empire, ruled from Istanbul. Until about 1750, textile manufacturers throughout Europe could obtain brilliant reds in wools and silks, but were confounded by cotton, which was more resistant to dye. Realizing that dye masters in the Levant, the areas east of Greece, knew how to color cotton a bright, fast red, European manufacturers sent industrial spies to bring home the secrets of Turkey red.

Antique quilt (detail), *Feathered Star* with redwork embroidery, by Sarah Maria Grizzel (1853–1914), estimated date 1880–1900, Barton County, Kansas. Collection of Mr. and Mrs. Elden Harwood. Turkey red and green on a white background was the standard palette for best quilts. The Turkey red cotton thread and outline-embroidered style of embellishment date to 1880 or later.

The dyestuff was madder root, a plant Europeans knew quite well, and one they used to obtain a variety of colors: browns, oranges, purples, and reds. But the only reds Europeans had produced were "sad" shades of burnt orange, cinnamon, and wine. The Eastern dyers' secret process for a fiery red involved more than a dozen steps over many months, including boiling the yarn in an oil mordant, a step described in another popular name for Turkey red cloth—oil-boiled calico. The process was also called "Adrianople red," after the Turkish city that was the major center of production.

British quilt historian Janet Rae quoted an advertisement from the *Glasgow Mercury* in 1785: "Dale and Macintosh have now got their Dyehouse finished, and are just begun to dye cotton yarn Turkey Red for the Manufacturers at large at 3 s[hillings] per lb. weight. The excellency of this colour is already known here." The process was designed for dyeing cotton in the yarn stage. Dale and Macintosh instructed cotton weavers to bring their yarn in four-pound hanks, tied together with a strong string on

which they marked their name. The dyers could then return the colored yarn to the proper owner, who wove it into bright red cloth, or mixed it with other shades for plaids and stripes.[10]

In the early nineteenth century, European chemists devised methods to add pattern to cloth woven from red yarn by discharging or bleaching out figures, first by applying discharge agents with woodblocks, later with rollers. The printers might simply design a pattern with a white figure on the red ground, or add a third color by printing a brownish-black with another block or roller. Turkey red prints grew more complex as calico printers determined how to add yellows and blues by modifying the discharge process. The overlap of yellow and blue produced green. Turkey red prints thus featured figures of white, chrome yellow, Prussian blue, overprinted green, and a brownish-black from logwood—color schemes dictated by the technology of discharge printing on a red-dyed cloth. Purples, oranges, pinks, and indigo blues did not figure into the color combinations.[11]

American quiltmakers formed a passion for Turkey red evident in thousands of surviving quilts made

Antique quilt top, coxcomb variation, signed "Mary A. Turley, 1869," by Mary Turley Morgan (1854–1917), fifteen years old, Indiana. Collection of Elizabeth Pett. Photograph courtesy of the Kansas Quilt Project. Note the border on only three sides, a common format. Double pinks often accented the red, green, and white color scheme. Appliquéd quilts with complex pattern and appliquéd border generally date from 1840 to 1870. This one was made at the end of the fashion. The lesson to be learned from the past: "Don't hide your light under a bushel. Appliqué your name on the front—in big letters."

after 1840. Seamstresses developed distinctive fashions based on a Turkey red color scheme. They used it for their best quilts with fancy quilting and corded bindings. They believed "genuine Turkey red" fabric was colorfast. It would not bleed in water; it did not fade in sun. Their faith appears well-founded because the fabric in their quilts remains vibrant a century and a half later.

Yet Turkey red cotton, whether printed or plain, has a fatal flaw. The complex dyeing process causes the red yarns to wear before most other fabrics in a quilt. Too many once-elegant appliquéd quilts are in poor condition due to shattered Turkey red.

Packaged dyes for home use appeared about 1880. Despite the label promising "Fast Turkey Red," this is probably Congo red, a synthetic dye that was quite fugitive. Turkey red is a process, not a powder, therefore a package of Turkey red dye is impossible.

Printing processes added to the deterioration. Chemicals used to bleach discharge-printed figures, and additional dyes, especially madder brown, can cause paisley cones and florets to rot away, leaving neat holes in the red background. Its fragility means that collectors should exercise extra caution with Turkey red cotton and avoid abrasion in use and cleaning. Agitation in a washing machine or a dry-cleaning machine can be remarkably destructive, causing the reds that have endured for generations to shred to mere threads.

Despite young America's fascination with Turkey red and a growing textile industry, American dyers and calico printers lacked expertise for the process described as "by far the most complicated employed in the whole art of dyeing." Americans who wanted fast, bright red calicoes for quilts and clothing bought imported fabrics until after the Civil War. In 1868, chemists imitating natural dyes in test tubes learned to synthesize alizarin, madder's coloring agent. Madder, worth fifty English pounds per ton, sold for eighteen within ten years, weakening the economies of India and countries where madder cultivation was a way of life.[13]

Synthetic alizarin simplified the Turkey red process, as dyer A. J. Hall explained: "Older methods of dyeing in which the natural dye was used required about four months. Modern methods allow fabric to be dyed within three days but this gain in speed is accompanied by a slight decrease in quality." With an easily industrialized synthetic dye, American mills launched domestic production. Plain red cottons made in the U.S. appear identical to earlier European imports, but post-war domestic Turkey red prints are noticeably inferior. Mills kept technology simple and costs low by printing only white or blackish-brown figures on bright red grounds.[14]

New synthetic reds like Congo red and neutral red appeared during the last decades of the nineteenth century, yet Turkey red cottons continued popular, despite their higher price. Mail-order catalogs often directed advertising to the quilt market, selling "comforter calico . . . in red grounds with combinations of black in scroll and oriental designs." The

RIGHT
*Reproduction quilt, *Prairie Sun* by Jean Pearson Stanclift and Cherié W. Ralston, 1999, Lawrence, Kansas, 87" x 87". Many quiltmakers view traditional red and green color schemes as too vivid to harmonize with the muted shades of today's country interior fashion. Jean and Cherié updated classic colors on an ecru figured ground with golden ochres, brick reds, and screen door greens. Their inspiration was a quilt made in Auglaize County, Ohio, about 1880.[12]

LEFT
Antique appliqué sampler, made by a Fitzsimmons family member, estimated date 1840–1865, possibly Jacksonville, Illinois, 80" x 85". Collection of Kern and Barbara Jackson. Appliqué patches are hand tacked with a fine buttonhole stitch over raw edges. The design seems a unique composition of blocks and border, but several nearly identical quilts have been discovered, made from West Virginia to Illinois, primarily along the fortieth parallel, the line of western migration across the United States. The lesson from the past to be learned here is the importance of a bold border, which really makes this quilt.[15]

RIGHT
Reproduction quilt, *Baby's Basket* by Karla Menaugh, 2001, Lawrence, Kansas, 42" x 35". Machine quilted by Pamela Mayfield. Karla refashioned an antique crib quilt with a softer palette.[16]

LEFT
Reproduction quilt, *Liberty's Eagle* by Karla Menaugh, 2001, Lawrence, Kansas, 40" x 40". Machine quilted by Pamela Mayfield. The inspiration was a quilt found in a trunk in Topeka, Kansas, years ago. The flags and the eagles with liberty caps resemble Baltimore Album-style quilts of the 1850s. Karla's one-quarter-size copy reflects today's folk/primitive colors, classic Americana updated.

1925 Sears, Roebuck and Company catalog spotlighted Turkey red's charms: "All women who make patchwork quilts know this good cloth. The bright cheery color forms needed contrast to make patchwork designs stand out sharply."

Dye houses developed more reliable synthetic dyes after World War I, offering at least 100 reds, most of them quite colorfast. The twentieth-century reds often have a characteristic orange cast—a tomato-red, not the bright cherry color of the classic Turkey red, which became obsolete during World War II.

Quilt styles associated with Turkey red lost favor in the early twentieth century as quilters lost faith in red fabrics and interior decorators swayed taste in quilts. Magazines offering new designs in new color schemes condemned old patterns and styles that had long passed from seamstress to seamstress. In 1926, *The House Beautiful* regretted that Turkey red quilts were "impossible to harmonize with the soft colorings of blue, rose and mauve . . . Quaint old quilts [are] perpetual white, or rather red, elephants on our hands." Quilt historian Ruth Finley wrote the epitaph in 1929. She described the old red, green, and yellow color schemes as unpleasant "enough to set a blind man's teeth on edge," using language insensitive enough to set our teeth on edge.[17]

Faded Reds

Antique fabrics and block dating from 1840 to 1860 in Turkey red prints in French Provincial style. The plain colored swatch could date from 1840 or 1925, as solid Turkey red is difficult to date. The prints with Turkey red grounds and figures of yellow, brownish-black, blue, and green are typical imports from France or Scotland, which also boasted a huge Turkey red printing industry. The gold foil label, once glued to a bolt end, advertises "Warranted Turkey red" and pictures a hookah-smoking Turk. A Pennsylvania woman preserved it between the pages of her account book of the 1840s (see page 50).

Reproduction fabrics in shades echoing pre-Civil-War Turkey reds. Figures, florets, and paisleys can be set or tossed. The swatch with paisley stripe to the left dates to the 1950s.

French Provincial Prints

Postcard, Madame Greder of Marseilles, France, posing in typical Provincial costume in 1906. She wears a quilted, floral-print skirt, a blouse in a *foulard* print, and a fichu or scarf of a bordered print in the *Indienne* style.

When seventeenth-century trade between East and West developed, Westerners prized printed cottons so highly that manufacturers of traditional European textiles of wool, linen, and silk responded to the foreign threat by restricting Indian cottons. Marseilles, a city on the Mediterranean Sea, was the only French port permitted to import these forbidden *Indiennes*. Entrepreneurs smuggled printed cottons into other parts of France, but it was in Provence, the province in which Marseilles is located, that they enjoyed the most popularity. Provençaux, the people of Provence, adopted *Indiennes* as their folk costume. Women farmers and tradespeople folded squares of border-printed fabric into triangular scarves called *fichus*, a form of scarf (*foulard*). They quilted the cotton prints into petticoats and topped the petticoats with printed skirts.

Textile mills in Provence learned to print their own versions of the *Indiennes* and now, 200 years later, Avignon and Arles are awash in French Provincial

Carte de visite, woman in a dress of a *foulard*-style print, probably a wool blend, about 1865.

prints. Tourists sleep under whole-cloth quilts and dine atop flowered tablecloths. Each open-air market features a booth with tablecloths, bags, clothing, and yardage of the bright, clear blues, warm yellows, and vivid reds. Like the *Indiennes* they imitate, *les tissus de Provence* (the fabrics of Provence) repeat naturalistic florals in border prints and patterned stripes. Today's yardage adds sunflowers and wheat to the stylized wild roses of the past.

One distinctive print style is a small isolated figure set in diagonal repeat. The figure may be a flower, leaf, paisley cone, or motif so abstract it is identified only as a *mignonette* (little fancy). The print style with

Carte de visite, woman in what looks to be a cotton dress.

marvelous. He praised "the equal distribution of the surface ornament over the grounds . . . the presence of so much unity of design . . . amid the general disorder everywhere apparent." Contrasting these spare, neat prints with more naturalistic English botanicals, he admired the stylized *mignonettes*, realizing "how unnecessary it is for any work of decoration to more than indicate the general idea of a flower."[18]

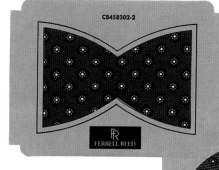
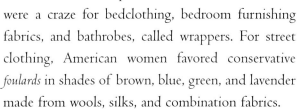

Classic silk *foulards* as necktie samples, about 1950.

its diagonal, neat design is known as a *foulard* or an *Indienne*, a French copy of an Indian-style print. In France and in the original Indian designs, the diagonal figures are often printed as fields within four borders of more naturalistic, undulating florals and vines.

Figures fall in a half-drop repeat with rows aligned in staggered fashion, giving the overall effect of a diamond grid. The look is spotty, especially when figures in the bright grounds are surrounded by white rings. The halo separating the figure from the ground was once necessary when colored grounds were woodblock additions, but today the halo is a style convention that defines French Provincial. Because these prints were so fashionable for scarves, the French word for scarf, *foulard*, came to mean any half-drop print of isolated small figures. Today's French Provincial fabrics are printed with synthetic dyes by rollers or screens rather than with the old woodblock technology and natural dyes such as Turkey red and Prussian blue.

English designer Owen Jones, upon encountering Indian fabrics at an 1851 exhibition, thought them

In the years between 1840 and 1865, Americans craved *foulards* to the point that they became a standard for American clothing and quilts. Bright cotton Provincial prints were a craze for bedclothing, bedroom furnishing fabrics, and bathrobes, called wrappers. For street clothing, American women favored conservative *foulards* in shades of brown, blue, green, and lavender made from wools, silks, and combination fabrics.

Between 1840 and 1880, American quiltmakers considered imported French Provincial cottons, especially those dyed in the Turkey red method, a necessity for floral appliqué and album quilts, both pieced and appliquéd. Why the bright blues and yellows, so popular in Provence, never caught fire with American quiltmakers is a mystery.

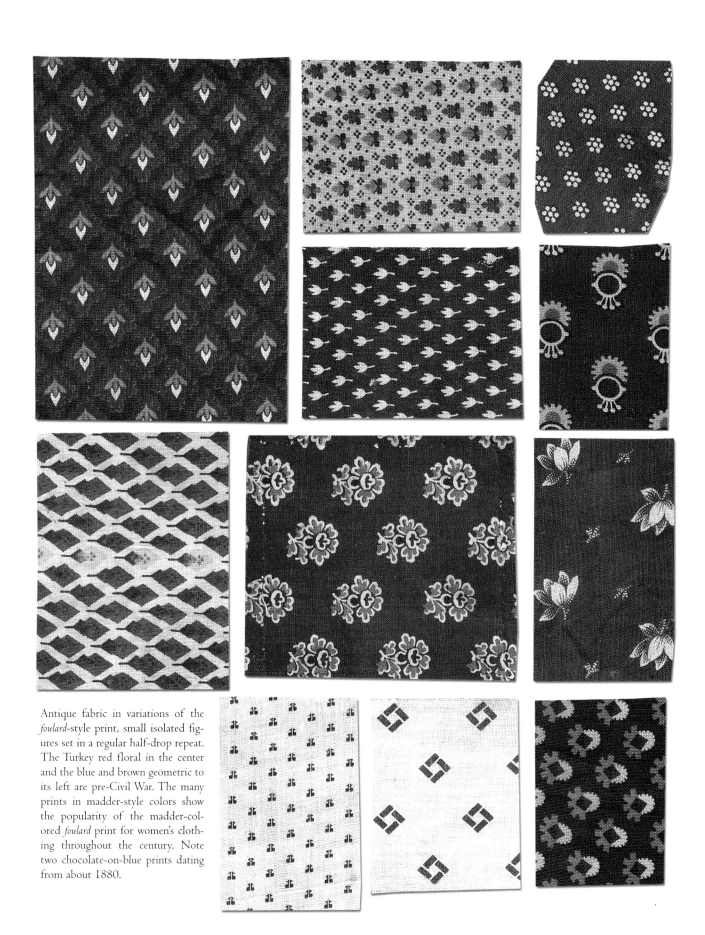

Antique fabric in variations of the *foulard*-style print, small isolated figures set in a regular half-drop repeat. The Turkey red floral in the center and the blue and brown geometric to its left are pre-Civil War. The many prints in madder-style colors show the popularity of the madder-colored *foulard* print for women's clothing throughout the century. Note two chocolate-on-blue prints dating from about 1880.

Reproduction fabric in *foulard*-style prints. Today's quilters generally prefer a tossed set to a regular *foulard*. We like figures to look scattered across the fabric rather than lined up in spotty rows. Orderly *foulards*, however, give an authentic look to mid-nineteenth-century reproductions.

Plaids

LEFT
Antique quilt top, *Wild Goose Chase* (detail), estimated date 1840-1860. Collection of Pam Johnson. High fashion cottons include rainbow prints, Prussian blues, printed plaids, checks, and stripes set with strips of printed plaid accented by rainbow shading.
RIGHT
Carte de visite, Cedarburg, Wisconsin, about 1865. The girls wear the typical fashions of the time, a plaid Balmoral skirt and a *foulard* print dress. Floor cloths and carpets in plaid designs were also in good taste.

The mid-nineteenth-century passion for plaids dates to the early 1840s when Queen Victoria and Prince Albert fell in love with Scotland and an old estate called Balmoral. Her diary from the Highlands reveals her love for Scotland's landscape and people, as well as their customs, many of which she adopted and popularized. To Queen Victoria we owe our taste for oatmeal porridge, Collies, Scottie dogs, and plaids (the word *plaid* is Scots for blanket).[19]

Woven from warps and wefts dyed different colors, plaids are labor-intensive and thus were expensive, so nineteenth-century textile mills offered many cheaper printed plaids. Printing plaids allows designs weaving never could. Mills printed plaids with designs impossible to weave, for example, wiggly lines or diagonal warps. Prints combined plaids and florals, plaids and stripes, plaids and figures, and even two different plaids into some wonderfully busy combinations. Printed plaids were more than cheap copies of woven design; they achieved a liveliness woven geometrics could never share.

Victoria was mad for plaid in decorating and dress. A court lady described the furnishings at the new Balmoral Castle in 1855: "The carpets are Royal Stewart Tartan and green Hunting Stewart, the curtains… the same dress Stewart, and a few chintz with a thistle pattern, the chairs and sofas in the

VIRGINIA, DECEMBER 1861

" *All the camps now seem to be filled with women, roving about and flaunting their bright dazzling Balmorals to the admiring gaze of the soldiers. They are the first I have ever seen of that style of dress.* "

DIARY OF ANNE S. FROBEL[20]

LEFT
Carte de visite, Rushford, Minnesota, about 1865. Printed plaids, unlike woven plaids, could have a diagonal orientation.
RIGHT
Carte de visite, Charlestown, Virginia, about 1865. Boy or girl in a Balmoral hat? The pantalettes are frilly, but the toy hoop indicates it's a boy.

Cabinet card, girl in a dress of printed plaid, about 1880. Printed plaids continued popular for clothing throughout the nineteenth century, but later plaids were not so bold as those of the pre-Civil-War years. Quiltmakers continued to use them but no longer flaunted them.

drawing room are 'dress Stewart' poplin. All highly characteristic and appropriate, but not all equally *flatteaux* to the eye."[21] (We needn't know French to read her disdain.)

While in Scotland, Victoria liked to wear a traditional wool shawl woven of the family tartan. Albert sported a complete Highland outfit of kilt, hat, and knee socks. In 1850, *Godey's Lady's Book* advised, "A woolen shawl . . . is indispensable to the toilette of every lady." Photographs of women in the 1840s reveal a style for bold plaid dresses that probably resulted from Victoria's much publicized trip to

Scotland in 1844. She also started a later fashion for the Balmoral skirt, described in her 1857 diary entry: "We started in 'Highland state,' Albert in a royal Stewart plaid and I and the girls in skirts of the same."[22]

Plaids in the scrapbasket wound up in quilts, so a bold, printed plaid is a good clue to a quilt made between 1840 to 1865. Printed plaids continued into the 1870s and beyond, but lost their bold color and scale. Woven checks and plaids are not as easy to date because the technology and style are so durable. However, plaids—woven or printed—were popular enough in this era that a simple dating rule is: "The more plaids, printed or woven, in the quilt—the closer to 1840–1865."

Shopping List for Fabric of Young America

- Prussian blue prints
- Rainbow prints
- Plaids, printed and woven
- Turkey red prints with yellow, brownish-black, blue and green figures
- Provincial prints with foulard-style sets

Reproduction quilt, *Antique Medallion* by Cherié W. Ralston, 1999, Lawrence, Kansas, 79" x 79". Cherié skillfully combined a variety of traditional patterns to create the style today's quiltmakers call the "folk/primitive" look. She added country coloring with lots of plaids and checks in a toned-down version of the traditional red, green, blue, and gold color scheme with tan for a neutral. Layering an appliqué vine over the seams is an updated design idea that ties the composition together.

The Fabric of Young America

Antique fabric, printed plaids ranging from 1830 to 1940. The newest piece is the diagonal plaid at top left in World War II shades of apple green and maroon. The oldest is the delicate floral-on-plaid ground at bottom right. The strangest features a purple zig-zag, about 1890.

Reproduction fabric, printed plaids. Swatches along the right side, though not marketed as reproductions, are wacky enough to look good in quilts hoping to capture the look of the 1840s, when fabric like the swatch at center bottom combining a floral stripe with a rainbow plaid was the latest in fashion.

Cactus Rose

Reproduction quilt, *Cactus Rose*, designed by Barbara Brackman, pieced by Pamela Mayfield, appliquéd by Jean Pearson Stanclift, hand quilted by Anne Thomas, 2002, Lawrence, Kansas, 50" x 50".

The more I've looked at French Indiennes and true India prints, the more I see a resemblance between fabric design and mid-nineteenth-century quilts like this one with blocks on point and vine borders. Blocks repeat in a regular diagonal grid, just like a foulard set. The image in the block is rather simple, a suggestion of a flower, a mignonette. Borders are organic, flowing in formalized vines like the borders on French neck scarves. Did the rage for Indiennes determine the look of our classic mid-century quilts?

FINISHED QUILT, 50" X 50"

FABRIC REQUIREMENTS

Plain white: 2½ yards of white with a slightly yellow cast, so it looks antique, will give you the traditional look for the background. Avoid unbleached muslin as its slubs and rough look are more twentieth century than nineteenth. *For a more updated look, mix and match light colored prints for the background: 1½ yards for the border and 4 blocks, 1½ yards for the edge triangles and 4 blocks, and 3 more fat quarters for the other 5 blocks*

Reds: ¼ yard each of 5 Turkey red Provincial reproduction fabrics (fat quarters are fine) and ¾ yard of a 6th red for blocks and binding

Greens: ¼ yard each of 5 fabrics (fat quarters are fine) and ¾ yard of a 6th green for the vine and leaves

BLOCK, 9" X 9" FINISHED

Backing: 3 yards
Batting: 54" x 54"

CUTTING

•Cut 2 border strips 6½" x 50¾" from the light background fabric for the top and bottom borders.

•Cut 2 border strips 6½" x 38¾" from the light background fabric for the side borders.

•Cut 2 large squares 14" x 14" from the light background fabric. Cut each square into quarters diagonally. This will give you 8 setting triangles for the sides.

•Cut 2 squares 7¼" x 7¼" from the light background fabric. Cut each square in half diagonally. This will give you 4 setting triangles for the corners.

BORDER, 6" FINISHED

•Cut 7 squares 7⅜" x 7⅜" from the light background fabric. Cut each square in half diagonally to make 14 triangles (D), 1 per block. You will have 1 extra triangle.

•Cut 10 squares 5"x 5" from the light background fabric. Cut each square in quarters diagonally to make 40 triangles (C), 3 per block. You will have 1 extra triangle.

•Cut 39 squares (B) 3⅛" x 3⅛" from the light background fabric, 3 per block.

•Cut 6 yards of binding (straight grain or bias) from the largest piece of red.

•Cut 4 red and 2 green diamonds for each block using a template made from pattern (A), 52 reds and 26 greens total.

• Cut 6 yards of ½" finished bias strip from the largest piece of green for the vine in the border.

• Cut 1 long stem (E) and 1 leaf (F) from green fabric for each block, 13 stems and 13 leaves total. Cut 24 stems (G) and 24 additional leaves (F) from green fabric for the border appliqué.

• Cut 24 flowers (H) from red fabric for the border appliqué.

THE QUILT TOP

(Patterns for the appliqué shapes and the feather quilting designs can be found on page 79, following project instructions.)

Blocks

1. For each block, prepare the stem (E) and leaf (F) for appliqué.

2. Baste, pin, or glue the stem to triangle (C), leaving the long end free.

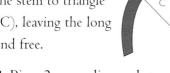

3. Piece 2 green diamonds to the triangle (C)/stem unit.

4. Sew 4 red diamonds together, then sew them to the green dia-

monds/stem units, tucking the raw edge of the stem into the seam.

5. Set in 3 squares (B) and 2 triangles (C) to make a block.

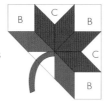

6. Add triangle (D) to fill out the block.

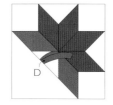

7. Pin, baste, or glue the rest of the stem (E) and the leaf (F) to triangle (D).

8. Appliqué the stem and leaf.

9. Set blocks into diagonal rows with side setting triangles pieced to each end, as shown.

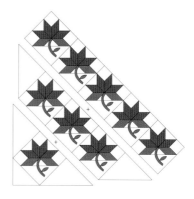

10. Join rows, adding the 4 corner triangles after the rows have been joined.

Borders

1. Add the side borders, then the top and bottom borders.

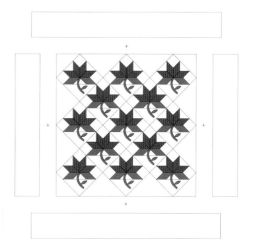

2. Turning under the edges of the stems (G), vine, leaves (F), and flowers (H).

3. Lay out the vine by placing a "hill" in the center of each border and a "valley" on either side of the hill. Pin, glue, or baste the vine and fill in the rest of the appliqué with the red flowers (H) and green leaves (F).

4. Appliqué the border.

Quilting

1. Use the vine in the border as the center to mark a feather around the border. Do not mark across the flowers or leaves.

2. Mark half a feather wreath in the 8 large side setting triangles.

3. Mark a small feather motif in the 4 corner triangles and at the intersections of the 4 center blocks.

4. Fill in background quilting by marking parallel diagonal lines 1" apart.

5. Layer and baste (page 125).

6. Quilt around the appliqué, either in the ditch or ⅛" away from each piece.

7. Quilt a line in the center of each leaf in blocks and border, and 3 lines in the border flowers, as shown on the templates.

8. Bind the quilt (page 126).

Valley   Hill   Valley

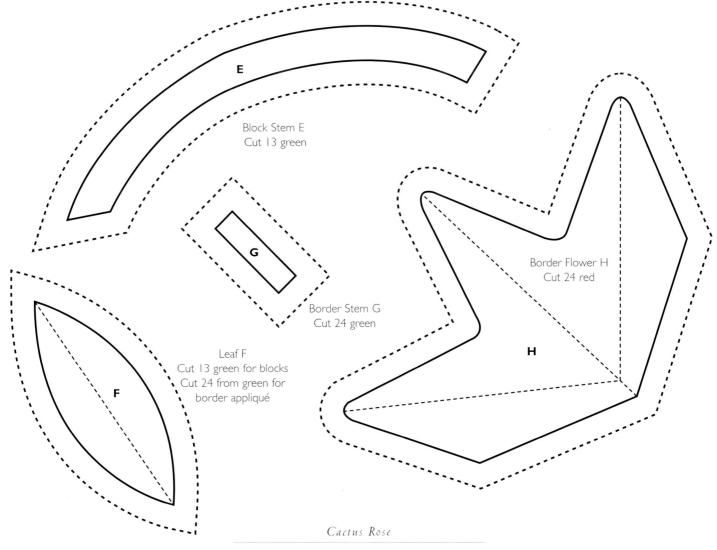

Block Stem E
Cut 13 green

Border Stem G
Cut 24 green

Leaf F
Cut 13 green for blocks
Cut 24 from green for
border appliqué

Border Flower H
Cut 24 red

Cactus Rose

79

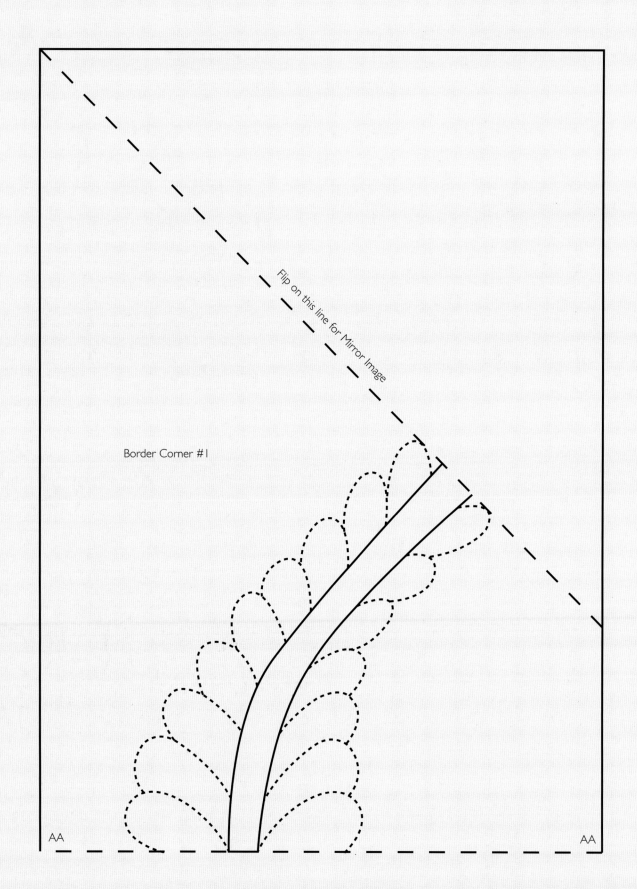

Flip on this line for Mirror Image

Border Corner #1

AA

AA

AA

AA

Side Border #2

BB

BB

Cactus Rose

81

BB
BB

Side Border #3

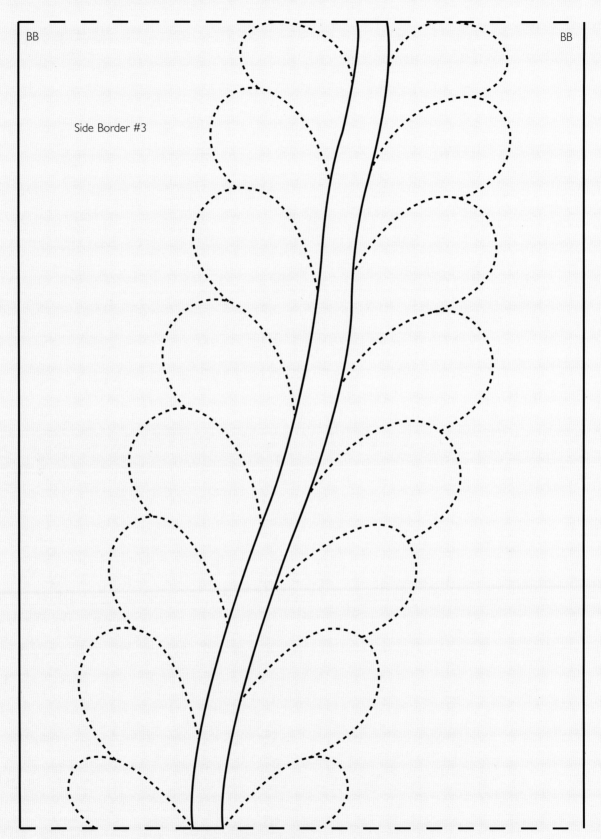

Flip on this line for mirror image on rest of border.

Half Wreath

A
Cut 4 red and 2 green for each block; 52 reds and 26 greens total

Small Feather Motif

Sawtooth Strip

Reproduction Quilt, *Sawtooth Strip*, by Barbara Brackman, 1992-2002, Lawrence, Kansas, 86" x 80". Machine quilted by Lori Kukuk.

I started this quilt, hand piecing it, years ago. One of my favorite reproduction prints is the blue and brown eccentric print in the setting triangles, from Pilgrim and Roy for P&B. The strips are an upholstery-weight fabric, really too heavy for a quilt, but I had to have the brown-ground chintz, so I bought the bolt. I emphasized Prussian blue and madder browns with pink and gold for accent.

If you examine the photograph you'll see I had trouble making the pieced strips the same size, primarily because I scissor-cut and hand pieced the blocks, so the block sizes varied. If you rotary cut and are careful with your ¼" seam allowance you won't have any trouble. Be careful about stretching the blocks when you join the strips. I was disgruntled when I saw the size variations in my strips, but when I looked at some old strip quilts, I realized I was not alone. Taking a lesson from the past, I added rectangles at the bottom of the strips where I needed to even things up. If you have to, think like a nineteenth-century quilter and cope as you can.

FINISHED QUILT, 86" X 80"   BLOCK, 10" X 5" FINISHED

FABRIC REQUIREMENTS

Chintz: 2½ yards for strips
Dark print: 2½ yards for triangle (A). I used an eccentric.
Light shirtings: ¼ yard each of a minimum of 8 fabrics for the backgrounds
Medium and dark prints: ¼ yard each of 15–20 fabrics. You should be able to get pieces for 4 to 8 blocks out of each ¼ yard.
Backing: 7 yards of chintz
Batting: 90" x 84"
Binding: ¾ yard

CUTTING

The instructions that follow will yield sufficient pieces for 4 blocks.

♦Cut I square 6¼" x 6¼" of the dark or medium print (C). Cut it in quarters diagonally, 4 large triangles, I for each block.

♦Cut 4 squares 3¾" x 3¾" of the dark or medium print (B). Cut each in quarters diagonally, 4 matching triangles for each block.

♦Cut 4 squares 2¼" x 2¼" from the dark or medium print (D), I per block.

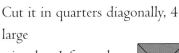

♦Cut 4 squares 3¾" x 3¾" from one shirting (B). Cut each in quarters diagonally, 6 matching triangles for each block.

Repeat 19 times to make a total of 80 blocks.

♦Cut 80 squares 5⅞" x 5⅞" from the dark eccentric print (A). Cut each in half diagonally, 160 total.

♦Cut 6 strips 6½" x 83" from the chintz setting strips. These are longer than you need, but trim them to fit when the pieced strips are finished.

THE QUILT TOP

Blocks

I. Piece triangular blocks as shown. You will be sewing on the bias edge, so handle carefully to minimize stretching the fabric.

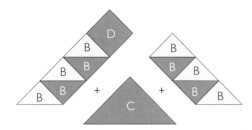

2. Add 2 triangles (A) of eccentric print to form rectangles.

3. Make 5 strips of 16 rectangular blocks each. Press.

4. Measure the length of the

pieced strips and trim the chintz strips to this measurement. Alternate the pieced strips with the chintz strips, beginning and ending with the chintz strips. Press.

QUILTING

1. Layer and baste (page 125).

2. Machine quilter Lori Kukuk used straight lines in old-fashioned elbow quilting. She marked lines down the middle of the chintz strips and made points 2½" apart. She quilted parallel lines that changed direc-

tion at those points, forming chevrons. One problem with straight lines is they accentuate inaccuracies in the piecing (I had *many*), but I decided to think like a nineteenth-century quilter and worry less about perfection. A contemporary look, and one that masks piecing problems better, is to quilt with curved lines, for example, meandering lines or vines in the strips.

3. Bind the quilt (page 126).

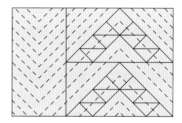

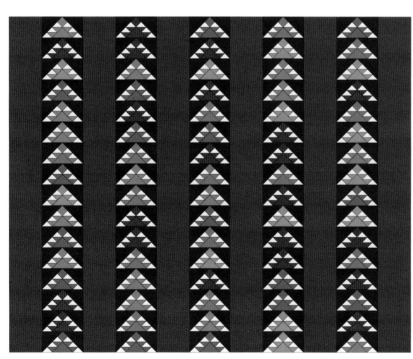

Quilt Diagram

Hickory Leaf

Reproduction quilt, *Hickory Leaf* by Barbara Brackman, 2003, Lawrence, Kansas, 94" x 94". Machine quilted by Lori Kukuk.

Appliqué is usually shaded in repetitive fashion, with all the leaves the same color. My inspiration was an 1870 scrappy appliqué quilt. I had a wonderful time finally cutting into the chintzes in my collection of reproductions.

"I saw more good hickory this day than in any former day of my life."
New York journalist Horace Greeley traveling in northeastern Kansas in 1859[23]

This quilt recalls an event in the days of the Kansas Troubles when settlers came to the Territory with pro-slavery or free-state convictions. In late 1855, Charles Dow, a free-state man from Maine, was shot by pro-slavery settlers from Missouri in a dispute over ideology and a land claim on a hill called Hickory Point, south of where I live. Dow's death set off a week-long skirmish called the Wakarusa War, which may be viewed as the first battle of the Civil War.

FINISHED QUILT, 94" x 94"   BLOCK, 20" x 20" FINISHED   BORDER, 7" FINISHED

FABRIC REQUIREMENTS

I updated the quilt by mixing printed backgrounds. I tried not to duplicate fabric for appliqué pieces in any block, but used 13 different reproduction prints in each. For that scrappy look you'll need at least 26 prints.

Light-background prints: 2½ yards each of 4 fabrics for blocks, and 2¾ yards of 1 fabric for border

Medium to dark prints: ⅓ yard each of 26 fabrics (fat quarters are fine)

Backing: 8 yards
Batting: 98" x 98"
Binding: ¾ yard

CUTTING

•From the large piece of background fabric, cut 2 strips 7½" x 94½" for the top and bottom borders. Cut 2 strips 7½" x 80½" for the side borders.

•Cut 4 squares 21" x 21" from each background print for the block backgrounds.

•Cut 4 each of appliqué shapes (A), (C), and (D) per block. You will need a total of 64 of each shape. (Patterns are on pages 89-90.)

•Cut 1 of shape (B) for each block.

THE QUILT TOP

Appliqué Blocks

1. Prepare the appliqué pieces by turning under the edges using your preferred method.

2. Press background fabric in quarters and then diagonally to create horizontal, vertical, and diagonal lines for placement.

3. Pin, baste, or glue the pieces in place.

4. Appliqué by hand or machine.

5. Trim the blocks to 20½" x 20½".

6. Sew the blocks into rows. Press.

7. Join the rows. Press.

Border

1. Add the side borders. Press.

2. Add the top and bottom borders. Press.

QUILTING

1. Mark a feather pattern in the border.

2. Layer and baste (page 125).

3. Quilt by hand or machine.

4. Bind the quilt (page 126).

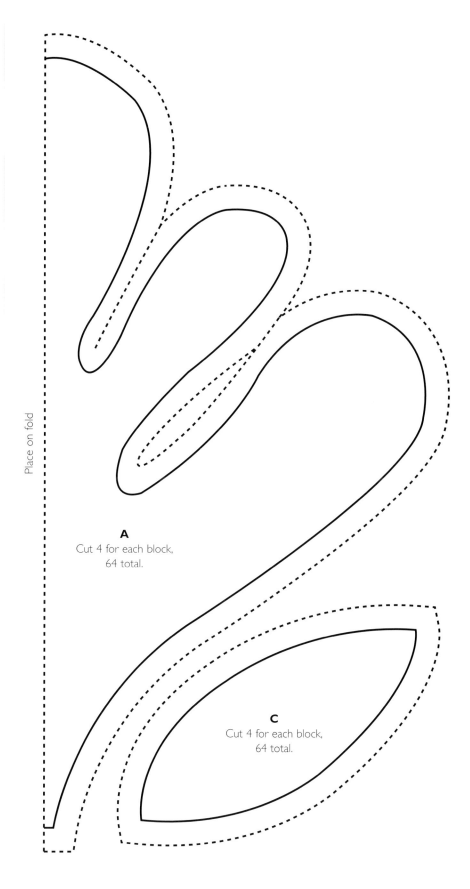

Place on fold

A
Cut 4 for each block,
64 total.

C
Cut 4 for each block,
64 total.

Hickory Leaf

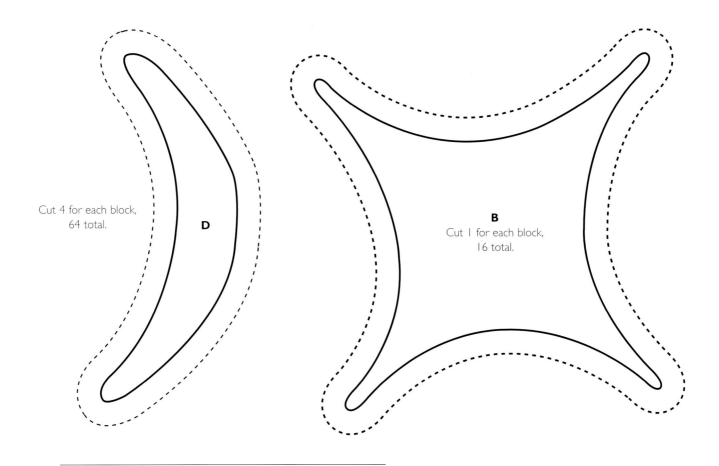

Cut 4 for each block, 64 total.

D

B

Cut 1 for each block, 16 total.

1 Larcom, *A New England Girlhood* (Gloucester, MA: Peter Smith, 1973) Pp. 203-204.

2 Thomas Dublin, *Farm to Factory* (New York: Columbia University, 1981) Pg. 100.

3 Ricky Clark, et al., *Quilts in Community: Ohio's Traditions* (Nashville: Rutledge Hill Press, 1991) Pg. 59.

4 J. N. Liles, *The Art and Craft of Natural Dyeing* (Knoxville: University of Tennessee, 1991) Pg. 48.

5 Rita J. Adrosko, *Natural Dyes and Home Dyeing* (New York: Dover, 1971) Pg. 20.

6 Martin Bide, "Technology Reflected: Printed Textiles in Rhode Island Quilts," Linda Welters and Margaret T. Ordonez, *Down by the Old Mill Stream* (Kent, OH: Kent State University, 2000) Pg. 111.

7 Hazel Clark, "The Design and Designing of Lancashire Printed Calicoes During the First Half of the 19th Century," *Textile History* 15 (I), 1984. Pp. 101-118.

8 Catherine Lynn, *Wall-paper in America* (New York: Norton, 1980) Pg. 507. Clark, Pg. 103.

9 Hugh Dunn Fisher, *The Gun and the Gospel* (Chicago: 1896) Pg. 150.

10 Janet Rae, *The Quilts of the British Isles* (New York: Dutton, 1987) Pg. 50.

11 Bide, Pp. 106-108.

12 Clark, et al., Pg. 28.

13 *A New Collection of Genuine Receipts for the Preparation and Execution of Curious Arts and Interesting Experiments.* (Boston: Charles Gaylord, 1831) Pg. 70.

14 A. J. Hall, *Dyes and Their Application to Textile Fabrics* (London: Sir Isaac Pitman & Sons, ca. 1935) Pg. 94.

15 Fawn Valentine, *West Virginia Quilts and Quiltmakers* (Athens: Ohio University, 2000) Pg. 76.

16 Dennis Duke and Deborah Harding, *America's Glorious Quilts* (New York: Hugh L. Levin, 1987) Pl. 143.

17 Elsie Marsh Brandt, "Red Quilts," *The House Beautiful*, Volume 60, November, 1926. Pg. 656. Ruth Finley, *Old Patchwork Quilts* (Philadelphia: Lippincott, 1929) Pg. 38.

18 Owen Jones, *The Grammar of Ornament* (London: B. Quaritch, 1868) Pg. 77.

19 David Duff, *Victoria in the Highlands* (New York: Taplinger Publishing, 1969).

20 Mary H. and Dallas M. Lancaster, *The Civil War Diary of Anne S. Frobel* (Birmingham, AL: Birmingham Printing, 1986) Pg. 69.

21 Dairy of Lady Augusta Bruce, quoted in Duff, Pg. 145.

22 Duff, Pg. 152.

23 Horace Greeley, *An Overland Journey* (New York: Knopf, 1964) Pg. 40.

Antique quilt blocks atop a reproduction quilt, a pattern called Joseph's Coat or Thousand Pyramids, which I started in 1991 when reproduction prints were uncommon. I soon abandoned my goal of making a true charm quilt with no two pieces alike, a fad in the 1880s. The paisley stripe in madder colors on the wall is from the mid-nineteenth century. The blocks are from the end of the century.

CHAPTER 4

Fabric of the Calico Craze
1865-1890

ATCHISON, KANSAS, FEBRUARY 15, 1887

" *The German ladies of the city gave a calico neck tie party at Turner hall [German gymnasium] last night. The ladies wore calico dresses, each depositing with the door-keeper a tie made out of the same material as their dress, which was drawn by one of the gentlemen, and the two were united for the evening. There was a great deal of fun about it all, and a great many ludicrous situations, which served to enhance the pleasure of the evening.* "

ATCHISON DAILY CHAMPION

LEFT
Tintype, woman in a calico dress, about 1870.
RIGHT
Invitation to a Calico Ball, February 20, 1874. Collection of the Kansas State Historical Society.

From the end of the Civil War to the end of that century, Americans were fascinated with small-scale dress prints, a fad they called the Calico Craze. Communities held calico balls, where women dressed in cotton dresses rather than the usual silk evening wear. Local fairs offered prizes for "the handsomest lady dressed in calico" and the prettiest "calico babies." Quilts from that era, the scrappy Log Cabins, Postage Stamps, and Ocean Waves, reflect the Calico Craze.

Small-scale prints were up-to-the-minute. Quiltmakers lost interest in large-scale prints as furnishing fabrics began to look "chintzy" and post-war tariffs on foreign

Cabinet card, Charles Rice, Fort Wayne, Indiana, about 1890. According to a note on the reverse, Mr. Rice stood as best man at a wedding. His three-piece suit with striped pants, plaid jacket, and vest looks to be made of Southern plaids.

the boudoir or within the confines of the family and close friends, was often made of calico. Wrappers and sacques were commonly stitched from the shirtings, paisleys, and stripes we see in the quilts of the day. In some areas, day dresses might be dark calicoes, but most women in cities continued to face the public in silk, wool, and combination delaines and challis.

After war-time scarcity, cotton prices dropped. In 1872, Montgomery Ward issued a two-page catalog, advertising cotton prints at twelve yards for a dollar. Fabric prices tumbled due to several factors. Technology improved dramatically with man-made dyes replacing the more expensive natural colors, and more efficient machinery replacing old. Competition increased, not only between American and foreign manufacturers, but also between North and South.

After the War, the ruined South had few assets besides future cotton crops. Realizing that the traditional system of trading raw material for manufactured cloth could never guarantee prosperity, a few Southern entrepreneurs decided to build mills to

yard goods increased the price differences between domestic and imported material. Calico quilts had a new look. Designs were more orderly than the old chintz quilts, contrast between darks and lights was more pronounced, and patchwork pattern predominated over prints. The rule became: "Complex patchwork, simple fabrics."

A new silhouette shaped women's clothing in the 1870s. No longer was a wide, round look in vogue. Women cut their bangs, frizzed them, and piled ringlets atop their heads to look tall and willowy. Fashion dictated gowns with draped skirts and bustles to exaggerate the rear view. Hand sewing yielded to the home sewing machine. The professional dressmaker was on her way to obsolescence. Fine handwork, the pride of earlier generations, followed.

Women's wardrobes reflected the availability of inexpensive fabrics as fashion and propriety demanded more changes of dress. Undress, the clothing worn in

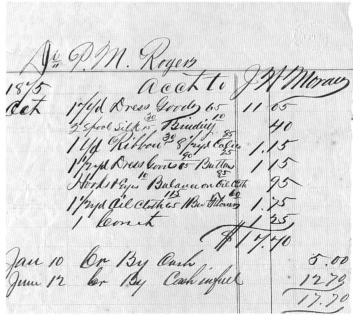

Account of Dr. P. M. Rogers at a dry goods store in Dresden, Tennessee, 1875. Mrs. Rogers bought dress goods at 65 and 85 cents a yard, calico at 25 cents.

LEFT
Cabinet card, Washington, Kansas, about 1880. Fashion demanded contrast in fabric texture, a taste reflected in the crazy quilts of the 1880s with their abundance of brocades, satins, and velvets. The photographer contrasted the heavy silk dress with a light calico throw.
RIGHT
Cabinet card, about 1890, a dress contrasting fabric rather dramatically while accentuating long, lean lines.

clean, spin, weave, and color the cotton. Among the most successful was Edwin Holt and his family. Holt began an empire in 1837 with his first mill in the area near Chapel Hill, now Alamance County. After Appomatox, Holt was determined to rebuild a Southern economy based on industry and capitalism rather than agriculture and slavery.[1]

Southern mill owners specialized in weaving coarse cotton cloth such as sheetings, tickings, drills, and jeans. They did not print the finer figured calicoes that required skilled printers, but focused on plaids and checks dyed in the yarn stage, then woven into pattern. The Southern plaids and checks, which became known as Alamance plaids, were the standard stuff of everyday clothing and household textiles in the South through the end of that century. Scraps of the Southern plaids wound up in many quilts and numerous Southern quilts survive with backings of Alamance plaid.[2]

The Southern fabric boom attracted the attention of New England mill owners only when they realized they were losing their traditional advantage. Southern mills wove enough cotton to supply their regional market, and then exported cloth to Europe and Asia. The South paid lower taxes, lower wages, and spent less on energy. They'd equipped new factories with new machinery, while Northern mills still operated with old equipment installed during the technological revolution of the 1830s.

New England conceded the market for coarse cottons to the South. The older mills began to focus on finer fabrics, hoping to occupy the niche Europeans had filled since the years before the Revolution. Innovations such as the Lowell School of Design, opened in 1872 to train Americans in designing woven and printed fabrics, attempted to discourage the age-old copying of European prints.

Cabinet card, general store, about 1900. Stores like this one supplied American women with fabric and sewing notions.

The increase in factories and efficiency continued to force down cotton prices. Too many mills produced too much plaid, causing a Southern economic slump in the 1880s. Overproduction of Southern specialty cloth motivated the Holts to form the Cotton Plaid Manufacturers' Association in 1884. Like OPEC today, which self-regulates oil production, the Plaid Manufacturers' organization only intermittently succeeded. Plaids continued to dominate Southern production at cheaper and cheaper prices.[4]

Over the long run, New England could not compete with Southern production costs. One by one, Merrimack, Cocheco, Hamilton, and other mills opened branches in the South, transporting printing skills and machinery below the Mason-Dixon line. By 1920, the South dominated cotton production, and northern mills began to shut down. The Depression finished most of them, leaving huge brick shells on the shores of New England's rivers. We see the process repeated today, as Asian mills take over the international cotton printing business, competing with cheap wages, sophisticated machinery, and a supportive economic climate.

Advertising card for Madame Demorest's dress patterns. Sized dress patterns costing 10 to 30 cents were a sewing innovation initiated by Ellen Louise Curtis in the 1860s. The combination of the sewing machine, inexpensive fabric, and patterns from companies like Madame Demorest's and Ebenezer Butterick's encouraged women to sew their own wardrobes. The results—a great many more scraps for America's quilts.

The Queen of Industry or The New South by Thomas Nast, 1882.

MARCH 8, 1870

" *Cotton spinning has been paying very well this year . . . and I expect making money fast on checks . . . there is more money in checks than anything else and no end to the demand.* "

LETTER FROM THOMAS HOLT [3]

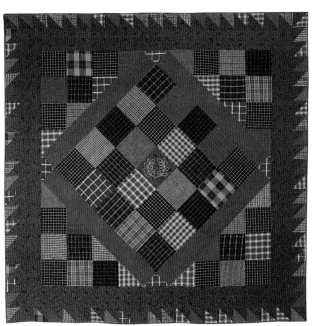

*Reproduction quilt, *Lee's Medallion*, pieced by Jean Pearson Stanclift, hand embroidered by Karla Menaugh, 2001, Lawrence, Kansas, 96" x 96". Machine quilted by Rosie Mayhew. This checkerboard was copied from a quilt made by Mrs. Robert E. Lee to raise money for a memorial to her husband, about 1870. Mary Custis Lee's quilt was pieced of wool and silk combination fabrics in plaids, stripes, and checks. We adapted the center diamond design to today's cotton flannels and embroidered a laurel wreath, the classical symbol of the hero. After the Civil War, Mary and General Lee lived in Lexington, Virginia, on the campus of Washington College, where he was president. When he died in 1870, she and friends made the quilt to raise a building fund for a chapel in his memory there. Her pattern is effective yet simple, a necessity because Mary Lee suffered from rheumatoid arthritis, which crippled her hands and confined her to a "rolling chair." The lesson to be learned from the past is "Any plaid goes with any other plaid."

Fabric of the Calico Craze

LEFT
Cabinet card, men and cotton bales, about 1900. A new force of Southern white laborers replaced the slave economy after the Civil War.
RIGHT
Cabinet card, Lucy Hamilton and her doll, Athol, Massachusetts, about 1880.

*Reproduction Quilt, *Union Square* by Pamela Mayfield, 2002, Lawrence, Kansas, 80" x 80". Rather than actually copying an antique quilt, Pam combined plaids and prints to evoke a post-Civil-War look. The lesson from the past is to contrast angular plaids and curvilinear prints in the same quilt, and use lots of browns for a period look. Pam updated the look by using borders as spacers and a frame. The first, narrow border of background fabric gives the blocks a little room to breathe. The second, dark border, what we sometimes call a "spacer" today, frames the piece. The last, wide border is in a neutral shade to echo the patchwork, again giving the design some space. In the last quarter of the nineteenth century, quiltmakers often pieced triple strip borders, but they rarely gave so much thought to actually framing the quilt as we do today.

CHARLOTTE, NORTH CAROLINA, OCTOBER 4, 1886

" *I one day saw a country merchant from Gaston, North Carolina higgling with a Charlotte dealer over a piece of Yankee plaids at 7 cents per yard. In a few minutes I saw the president of the McAden mill clad in a full suit of his own beautiful goods far superior to the other at 6¼ cents per yard.* "

THE BALLOT

Antique fabric of plaids and checks from the end of the nineteenth century: The long blue and white piece at top right, cut from clothing, is a linen homewoven check, purchased in Pennsylvania, where women continued spinning and weaving into the twentieth century. The other fabrics, all cotton, are likely factory-made. We might describe the pattern in the brown check at the center as "gingham," but in the nineteenth century gingham was a general term for cotton fabric dyed in the yarn stage—print, plain, or check. An old term for the fabric is "apron check."

Fabric of the Calico Craze

Reproduction fabric, woven plaids, stripes, and checks. Many of the new wovens are combed on one side. Combed cottons have long been called flannel. Woven designs have changed little over the centuries. A check might date to 1790 or 1990. For reproductions, look for classic colors of madder reds and browns, indigo blues, and black (after 1890).

Madder-Style Prints

Madder is a vegetable dye derived most efficiently from a perennial plant with the Latin name of *Rubia tinctorum*. Like many dye plants, it is an Asian native. James Liles traced madder's discovery to 2000 BC. Pliny the Elder, a Roman naturalist who traveled to Asia in the first century AD, described the amazing transformation of a piece of cloth treated with colorless mordants emerging from the dyebath in a rainbow of shades. The plant and its secrets traveled to Europe where madder thrived in Italy, France, Holland, and Spain. Other names for the dye are *al izarin* in Arabic and *garance* in French.[4]

ABOVE
Tintype, about 1865. Post-war dresses of narrow, neat stripes are possibly shades of madder.
LEFT
Carte de visite, about 1870.

Cottons dyed with madder are among the most common fabrics in nineteenth-century quilts. Madder pleased both mills and customers because it was colorfast and inexpensive, yet versatile. The calico printer treated the yardage with different mordants (metal salt solutions such as iron or aluminum) and dipped the cloth in a single dye bath made from madder root. Each mordant reacted differently with the dye, producing colors ranging from red-orange through purple, brown, and almost black. The madder coloring agent would not bind to areas that were not mordanted.

" *Piecing the Quilt*
 . . . A bit of blue in the center there,
 From a remnant left of her Sunday gown;
 A strip of white and a rose-pink square,
 And a border here of chocolate brown . . . "

HATTIE WHITNEY, GOOD HOUSEKEEPING, MARCH 1888

Growing conditions in America seemed ideal for madder. As the American textile industry developed, several influential farmers, including Thomas Jefferson, advocated madder cultivation. In 1823, William Partridge wrote in his dye manual: "Madder grows well in the western country and I am informed it thrives in all parts of the United States where it has been planted. Many farmers in Kentucky raise it for sale." Despite early optimism, America throughout the nineteenth century imported much of its commercial madder, primarily from India and Turkey. In 1864, agriculturists at New York's American Institute discouraged an Indiana farmer who inquired about planting a crop. "We think as a general thing, growing madder has not been successful in this country . . . an experiment in trying to grow madder in New Jersey [was] a complete failure. I believe all attempts to grow madder in this country have failed."[5]

During those years, chemists worked to make madder cultivation obsolete. European scientists learned to create dyes from coal tars, a waste product of burning coal. In 1868, Germans discovered a formula for synthesizing madder, an event important to chemistry as well as commerce. *Al izarin*, its name derived from the Arabic word, was the first manmade copy of a natural dye. These coal-tar dyes, also called analine dyes, provided dyers and printers with coloring agents of consistent strength that required no preparation to remove woody waste or other by-products. Less expensive, synthetic madder inevitably forced farmers to switch to other crops. Between 1868 and 1876 British imports of madder root fell by three-quarters and the price dropped by two-thirds.[6]

Textile manufacturers used the term "madder-style" to refer to madder's mordant printing techniques as well as to its palette. In his 1887 dye manual, Antonio Sansome described the spectrum of "old Madder Styles" with a bit of nostalgia: "reds, pinks, browns, purples, chocolates, blacks."[7]

Madder could produce brilliant Turkey red if it were mordanted and treated in a complex fashion, but Sansome was referring to simpler reds ranging from red-orange through brick red to wine, shades that dyers called "sad reds." Pinks, on the other hand, could be quite bright, the double pinks were so common in quilts and children's clothing in the nineteenth-century. But because the process to obtain bright pinks was different, pinks are not usually included under the term "madder-style prints."

Historian Lewis Mumford called the last years of the century "the Brown Decades." "The color of American civilization abruptly changed. By the time the war was over, browns had spread everywhere: mediocre drabs, dingy chocolate browns, sooty browns that beiged into black." His perspective, looking backward, reveals a twentieth-century disdain for the color, but in the gilded age, the era of brownstone buildings, walnut furniture, and chestnut-haired beauties, brown truly reigned. The most popular browns in cotton were madder shades—warm, reddish browns ranging from tan through dark, purplish brown the dyers called chocolate, the same shade as today's Hershey Bar wrapper. The American Museum of Textile History owns a handwritten dye book titled *Recipes For Chocolates*, which

Dye recipes and quilt by Grandmother Bissell, handed down in the family of quilt historian Ruth Finley. The quilt, from about 1850, shows wear typical of madder-dyed browns, especially in the triangles to the right of the book. The iron that mordants the coloring agent, making it fast, has a tendency to oxidize over time. The fabric is essentially rusting away. Madder browns are usually the first fabric to deteriorate in a nineteenth-century quilt.

has nothing to do with the edible kind. Another name for that purplish-brown is *puce*, Latin for flea, a name that supposedly dates to the days of Louis XIV, when French courtiers lived in close quarters at Versailles under extremely unsanitary conditions. Puce, considered both fashionable and functional, was the exact color of a flea. The vermin, live or crushed, wouldn't show on a court lady's dress.[8]

The purples Sansome mentioned were flat lavenders common to calico prints in American quilts, described in more detail below. Madder blacks are a dark brown rather than a true blue-black, and the quilt detective must learn the difference between madder's brownish-black and later sulfur black, which appeared after 1890. Madder black, usually used as figure rather than ground, has a reddish value, and sulfur black, which can be figure or ground, is more neutral.

" *The first calico printing done in Lowell was [at] the Merrimack Corporation, and the prints were of very poor texture and color. The groundwork was madder, and there was a white spot in it for a figure; it cost about thirty cents a yard. This madder-color was the product of an extensive cowyard in the vicinity of the print-works, and the prints were 'warranted not to fade.' I had a gown of this material, and it proved a garb of humiliation, for the white spots washed out, cloth and all, leaving me covered with eyelet-holes. This so amused my witty brother than, whenever I wore it, he accused me of being more 'holy than righteous.'* "

Harriet H. Robinson[9]

Madder browns and near-blacks have an unfortunate tendency to deteriorate or "tender" fabric. Iron used in the mordanting process interacts with oxygen in the air, essentially rusting the fabric over time. Antique quilts are full of madder-style prints that have oxidized, leaving holes in calicoes and empty lines in stripes. Many brown patches have completely disappeared. The darker the brown, the more iron in the mordant, and the more likely the fabric is to rot over time.

Madder-style prints combined reds, browns, oranges, and purples in small- and medium-scale prints. They were exceptionally popular in the decades after the Civil War, when madder prints were the standard for women's and children's casual dresses and men's and women's wrappers. Large paisley prints and wide stripes appear to be most common in quilts between 1850 and 1880; smaller, neat stripes were fashionable in the 1870s and 1880s. One quite specific fad for madder was a chocolate figure on a pale gray-blue ground, prints quite common in the 1870s and 1880s. By the 1890s, madder shades and madder-style prints looked dated, replaced by greener browns in manganese-bronze prints. The bronze-style prints combined a khaki-colored brown with olive, rose, and ivory white. To quiltmakers choosing fabrics at the turn-of-the-last-century, the reddish-brown, madder-style prints must have seemed terribly unfashionable. The Brown Decades were over.

Antique fabric in madder-style prints from the nineteenth century. The oldest are the large-scale leaf at the top left and the palm-leaf print to the immediate right, possibly 1815–1840. The newest are the chocolate brown and gray-blue prints along the bottom, which were very popular in the 1880s. That chocolate brown with a reddish tint is what people used to call *puce*.

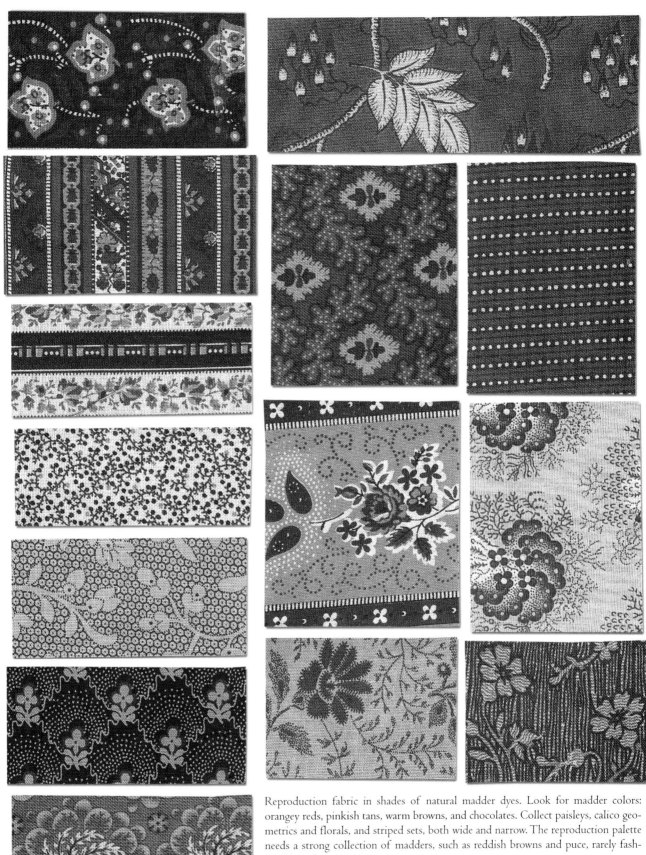

Reproduction fabric in shades of natural madder dyes. Look for madder colors: orangey reds, pinkish tans, warm browns, and chocolates. Collect paisleys, calico geometrics and florals, and striped sets, both wide and narrow. The reproduction palette needs a strong collection of madders, such as reddish browns and puce, rarely fashionable today.

Stereograph, about 1875. Stereo cards often featured quilts in humorous bedroom scenes. The woman wears her night dress, a wrapper made of striped cotton, probably in madder-style shades. The newly fashionable bed is completely open with a carved wooden headboard for decoration.

MORDANTS + MADDER—THE DYE CHEMISTRY

Alum (aluminum) mordant + madder = reds, pinks

Iron mordant + madder = purplish browns and blackish browns

Iron mordant + alum mordant + madder = chocolate browns

Add quercitron (another vegetable dye that produced different colors with different mordants) and the dyer obtained the red browns and cinnamon oranges.

With synthetic alizarin, tin mordants were used.

Purples and Mauve

A significant event in the history of science and technology was the discovery of synthetic purple dye by Englishman William Perkin in 1856. Perkin, a young chemistry student, hoped to duplicate the medicine quinine with coal gasses. Natural quinine was so expensive that millions of people around the world suffered from malaria because they could not afford the medication. Perkin's teacher August Hofmann theorized that an industrial pollutant derived from coal processing might be manipulated to yield a chemical similar to quinine.

Perkin's experiment in pharmacy failed, but he was astute enough to realize that the dark powder he produced could color a piece of silk a brilliant purple. Before long, he and his father were manufacturing a new dye, called mauve, from a French word for purple. Three years later London was in the grip of "Mauve Measles" with everyone from the Princess of Wales to the housemaids wearing mauve.[9]

Perkin is credited with inventing the first man-made coloring agent. Mauve and its chemical relations eventually replaced the natural purples that had dyed wool, silk, and cotton. As with all advances in dye technology, decades passed before the new faster, brighter, synthetic purples appeared in American quilts. At first the synthetic dyes were economically feasible only for expensive silks and woolens. Cottons continued to be dyed with natural dyes through the end of the century.

Purple was always one of the most difficult colors to obtain with natural dyes. Even when colorfast, the shade was a rather flat lavender, a color we see often in nineteenth-century quilts. Purple cotton calicoes usually feature two or three shades of purple, sometimes with a white or brownish-black figure. The dyers called the print style "double purple" or "two purples" and obtained it with either madder or logwood, a dye derived from a South American tree.

WASHINGTON, SEPTEMBER 12, 1864

" *Some very interesting experiments have lately been made by Dr. Henry Erol, Chemist of the Department of Agriculture, in testing the coloring matter in coal oil, and some sorghum seed. By combinations with different chemicals he finds that a great variety of colors can be produced from each of these substances ... There are different tints of purple also, and the beauty of them is that they are 'fast colors,' in the old-fogy-time meaning of that expression before fast people came into date.* "

CORRESPONDENT LOIS BRYAN ADAMS, DETROIT ADVERTISER AND TRIBUNE[10]

James Liles noted that old dye recipes he studied abound with logwood purples, which produce purples similar to madder purples. Logwood purple was expensive to produce, however, and no more light fast than the madders. "The dye fades from a very nice reddish purple to a rather ugly off-brown." Quilt collectors are familiar with the way some purples develop spots of brown that enlarge as time goes by. Many a nondescript brown patch in an old quilt might have been purple when new.[11]

Perkin's mauve had little immediate effect on calico quilts, although his discovery eventually transformed everything. At the most basic level, he gave the Western world new shades of a very desirable color. In the broader picture, chemists had learned how to concoct coloring agents in the laboratory rather than relying upon agriculture and mining for natural dyes, medicines, and flavors. Perkin opened the way for a world of chemical synthesis, the reason Simon Garfield's biography of Perkin, published in 2000, is called *Mauve: How One Man Invented A Color That Changed The World*. (A footnote—it wasn't until 1944 that scientists synthesized quinine.)

Antique quilt in a Variable Star pattern, unknown maker, about 1840–1890, 84" x 76". *"Sarah help[ed] me quilt on my diamond quilt that I pieced 18 or 20 years agone."* Like Emily Hawley Gillespie, who wrote those words in her diary in Manchester, Iowa, in 1877, the maker of this quilt might have started it twenty years or more previously. Most of the blocks look to be pre-Civil War, with large-scale prints and the buff and blue combinations popular in the 1850s. The set, on point with dark triangles framing the design, also echoes pre-War taste. Notice how badly those madder brown triangles are deteriorating. But the small-scale calico setting blocks of madder orange, the sparse quilting, and the backing fabric, which is the chocolate-on-blue style of print so popular in the 1880s, mark this piece as old blocks quilted later.[12]

If you look closely, you can see that the maker cut many of the large triangles in the star blocks a bit short. Undeterred, she cut little strips, pieced them onto the triangles, and didn't seem to care if anyone noticed. Some of the strips (I've heard people call these "coping strips" today) are bright green next to an indigo triangle. The lesson here is that quilts need not be perfect. This one's perfectly charming.

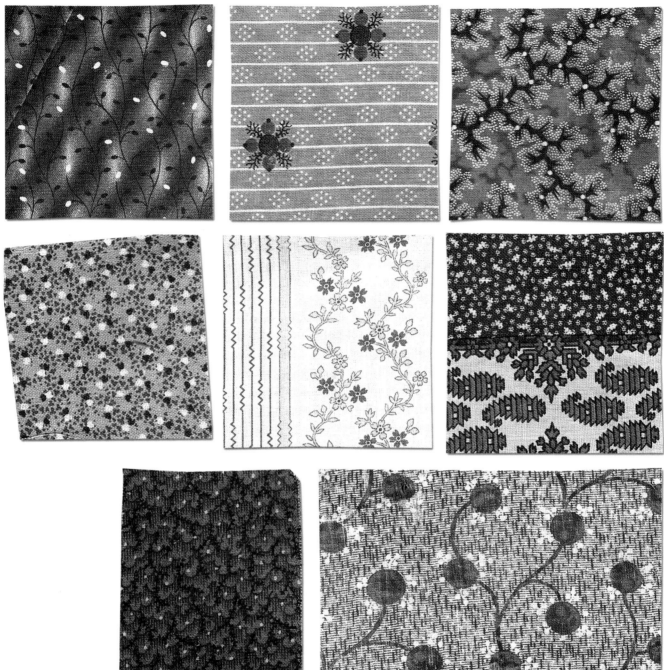

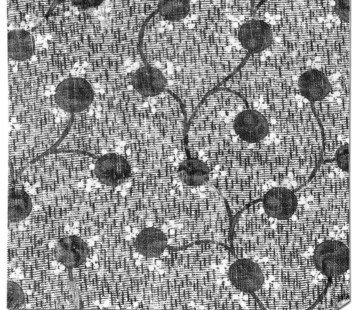

Antique fabric and blocks dating to 1845 through 1900. Unused fabrics are often brighter than the purples seen in finished and used quilts. Purples often turn brown in ever-widening spots. Is it light or oxygen that breaks down these natural dyes?

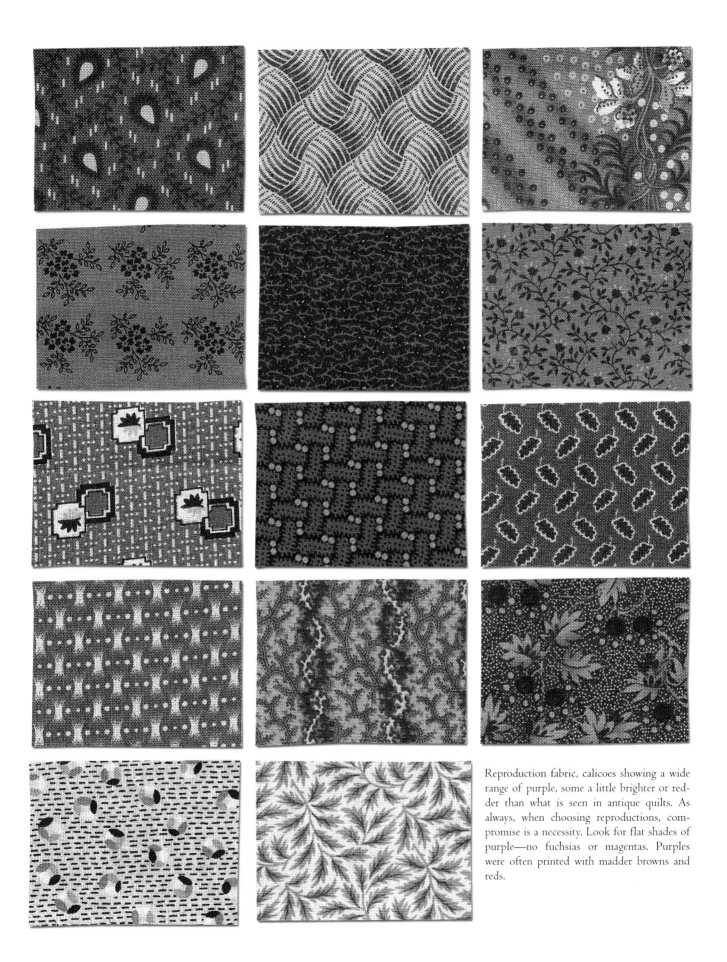

Reproduction fabric, calicoes showing a wide range of purple, some a little brighter or redder than what is seen in antique quilts. As always, when choosing reproductions, compromise is a necessity. Look for flat shades of purple—no fuchsias or magentas. Purples were often printed with madder browns and reds.

Paisley Prints

Antique quilt, detail of a comforter set with a paisley robe print, about 1910. Paisleys continued fashionable for bedding and bedclothing into the twentieth century. The patchwork block has over twenty published names. Two of the earliest are Double Wrench, printed in *Farm and Fireside* magazine in 1884, and Wrench from the *Ohio Farmer* in 1896.

LEFT

Carte de visite, woman in a paisley shawl, Inverness, Scotland, about 1865.

Paisley is an adaptation of traditional Indian textile patterning. About 1500, weavers in Kashmir began making shawls in this style, using wool from Himalayan cashmere goats. To relieve their itches, the goats rubbed against trees, leaving a fine wool that weavers gathered and wove on hand looms into shawls so fine a good one could be pulled through a wedding ring.

" MARYLAND, JANUARY 11, 1819

Please tell me the price of your Kashmir shawls, whether they are pretty, and whether you have any from France that are less expensive but still nice. The ones they are wearing here from India are outrageously expensive—from $400 to $600— and to me not attractive. "

LETTER FROM ROSALIE STIER CALVERT TO HER SISTER IN FRANCE[13]

The woven textiles had a face and a reverse. The Kashmiris sandwiched two shawls together and wore a pair of shawls (*shal* is Hindi for woolen covering). A weaver might spend five years on one piece, adding extra embroidery to the tapestry twill weaving. By the mid-eighteenth century, England's East Indian Company was importing shawls to London. Kashmir shawls became a fashion rage among the truly wealthy. One shawl might cost the equivalent of a house in London. They became a wearable symbol of status, the way a sable fur coat identified a rich man's wife in the 1950s.

The Industrial Revolution was all about factories imitating handwork, and the Kashmir shawl was one of the great successes. By 1840, Europeans were imitating shawls on automated Jacquard looms in factories in Lyons, Rheims, and Norwich, but the best shawls were made in the town of Paisley, on the west coast of Scotland. Paisley shawls were woven of fine worsted wool wefts crossing warps of silk spun with imported cashmere. The original Indian shawls featured a good deal of white, but Europeans preferred wools dyed in shades of madder browns ranging from dark chocolates to orangey reds, so the later manufactured shawls were darker than the handmade Kashmiri shawls. Factory-made shawls were priced within reach of the new middle classes, and in the mid-nineteenth century everyone wore them, including Queen Victoria and Abraham Lincoln.

The characteristic figure in the shawls woven by hand in India or by machine in Europe was a stylized botanical form, an oval shape with a curl on the end, known as a *botha* or *boteh* (from the Hindi *buta* for flower). The botanical source for the *boteh* design is in some dispute. A few textile historians see it as a pinecone, others a gourd or the shoot of a date palm.

By 1830 the cone shape, soon to be known as a paisley after the Scots town, was popular in cotton prints. The cone shapes could be spaced in regular repeats, as in the French Provincial patterns, or confined to striped sets. The *boteh* could curl around each other in an allover print. Women generally wore paisley cottons for intimate apparel rather than streetwear. The Oriental-looking designs, often printed in the madder shades of the original shawls, were popular for wrappers, the uncorseted clothing worn within the family circle. Paisleys, also called shawl prints, were fashionable for bedroom furnishings, one reason they are so common in quilts of the era.

About 1870, paisley shawls became old hat, and in 1886, the last true paisley shawl was woven in Scotland. Taste in cottons changed, too, and in the 1890s quilters favored geometrics and florals in blues and blacks over warm, reddish-brown paisleys. Thus paisleys in madder-style colors are a good clue for the quilt detective, indicating a quilt made before 1890.

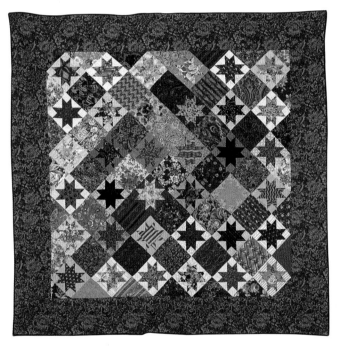

Reproduction quilt, *Lost in the Stars* by Georgann Eglinski, 2000, Lawrence, Kansas, 96" x 96". Machine quilted by Shirley Greenhoe. Georgann's inspiration, a quilt made about 1885, is in the collection of the Los Angeles County Museum of Art. The original makes the most of large-scale *cretonnes*, the furnishing fabrics of the 1880s, prints ignored by most quilters of the era. Georgann and friends made several quilts as a group project. They weren't interested in copying the original, but wanted to capture its style. Each woman pieced stars and met to trade blocks and share large-scale prints for the setting squares. They used several paisleys among the stripes and botanicals. The border is a reproduction of a print designed by Englishman William Morris. Morris's late-nineteenth-century designs, echoing medieval art, held little interest for American quiltmakers.[14]

Cabinet card photograph, about 1890. Interior fashion demanded a "Turkish corner" with a fabric tent, throw pillows, and a bit of paisley for an ethnic look.

Antique fabric and block from the last half of the nineteenth century. The paisley-style figures are set all-over fashion and in striped sets. Madder-style shades were popular for paisleys or shawl prints, because paisley shawls were dyed with madder, yet paisley prints appeared in any shade possible to dyers. The rather bright purple paisley at the lower right is turn-of-the-nineteenth-century, and may not be colorfast. The black scraps on the left are cut from a border print, typical of the 1890s.

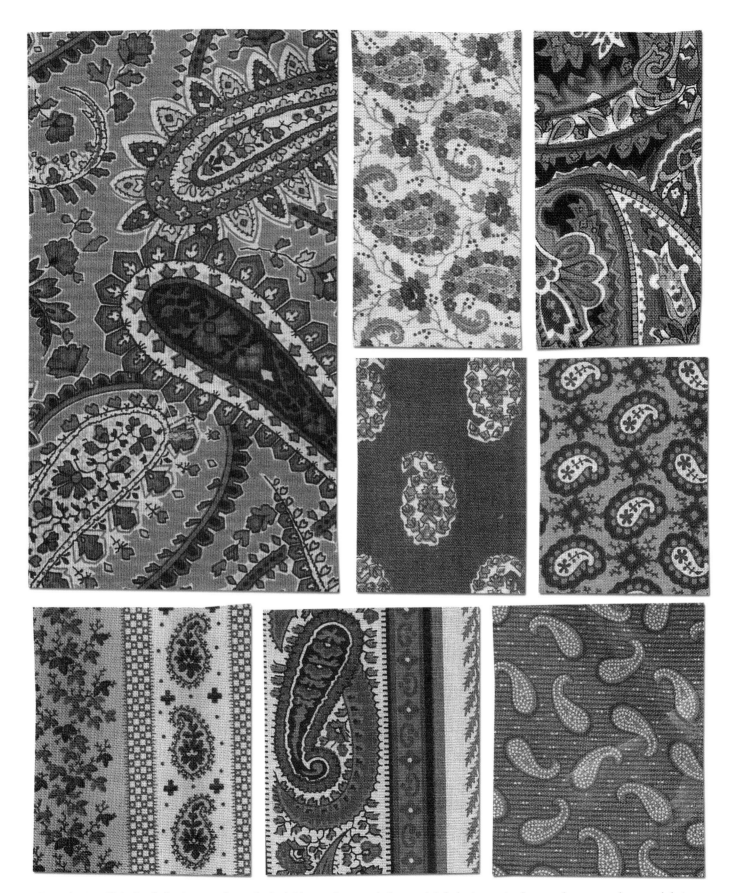

Reproduction fabric. Look for the cone shape, the *boteh*. Here we have regularly spaced *foulard* prints, striped sets, and more casual scattered designs. Layered designs place pattern atop pattern.

Shirtings and Mill-Engraved Conversation Prints

Cabinet card, Steubenville, Ohio, about 1910. Quilts and children's clothes shared much of the same fabric. The boys are wearing an anchor print, white on a dark ground.

Shirtings are light-weight, light-colored cottons popular for men's and children's shirts and lady's waists (blouses). Shirtings usually feature small florals or geometric figures, set rather sparsely on a white ground.

It is always a pleasure to come upon a conversation print while examining an antique quilt. The subject matter and detail give us something to talk about, which must be where these prints got their name. Conversation prints or conversationals highlight figures of recognizable objects other than flowers. In the nineteenth century, when shirtings showed sporting motifs, sewing tools, political images, and insects, refined company was obligated to make proper conversation. Home decorating might feature

a "conversation piece," a painting with an implicit story that could be discussed by visitors to the parlor. Garden vistas focused on an unusual object about which the conversation could develop in the same way a conversation print captures our attention in a quilt.

The term "mill engraving" refers to the printing technique for some of these finely drawn, light-weight cottons. In this case, the word "mill" does not mean the textile factory, but rather the old die-and-mill technology introduced in the early nineteenth century. Machine-cut metal dies defined steel or zinc mills, which in turn impressed copper plates for printing. The first fashion in mill engravings were fancy machine grounds in the 1820–1840 era. After 1870, mill-engraved conversation prints were stylish, as the

Antique quilt top, hexagonal design, about 1895, 37" x 50". Light colored shirting prints contrast with darker dress calicoes. By this point, taste had changed, dismissing reddish-brown madder prints. This quilt top makes use of several brown prints in the new manganese-bronze style, which gives a colder, almost grayish look to this piece. The lesson we can learn from the past is to mix and match prints for neutrals and backgrounds. At the dawn of the twenty-first century, we know this lesson well. Prints add detail and texture to the negative space in a design.

technology became inexpensive enough that textile factories could print quirky designs like bees or flies, patterns that did not promise to be big sellers.

Earlier quilts showcase rarer scraps featuring line drawings. An 1846 textile book includes a swatch featuring the head of a dog tipped-in (glued onto a page) and the Smithsonian Institution owns an early nineteenth-century quilt with an anchor print.[15]

During the latter part of the nineteenth century, at the same time that the mill-engraved conversational shirtings were popular for clothing and quilts, factories also produced conversation prints featuring white figures on Turkey red or indigo blue grounds. The dark prints, which were quite popular for children's clothing, appear in quilts from about 1880 through 1920. They rarely show the detail of the mill engravings, and are primarily sporting prints, another subcategory of conversationals. Anchors and sailing images, horseshoes, and racing equipment are common in these red and blue shirtings.

*Reproduction quilt, *Centennial Block* designed by Terry Clothier Thompson, pieced by Pamela Mayfield, machine quilted by Rosie Mayhew, 2001, Lawrence, Kansas, 60" x 84". Terry picked the block for its name, an old design that celebrates our 1876 anniversary, and then she chose fabric to reproduce the look of the 1870s. Conversationals and other shirtings were very important to quilt style 125 years ago.

Stereograph, about 1910, a technician at Lowell's Pacific Mills demonstrating how a hand-painted design for a large-scale print is transferred to the copper roller using pantography, a copying device. Smaller-scale prints such as conversationals were transferred to the copper rollers by a steel mill.

Shopping List for Fabric of the Calico Craze

- *Brown prints in warm, reddish browns (madder)*
- *Shirtings*
- *Conversation prints*
- *Stripes (narrow and neat)*
- *Paisleys*
- *Woven checks and plaids*
- *Dull purple prints*

Antique fabric, shirting prints of geometrics, simple florals, and leaves on white grounds. Figures were pinks, reds, blues, purples, browns, and (after 1890 or so) true blacks. Printers often combined two colors on white. The bright blue figures, almost blue violet, probably colored with Prussian blue dye, were fashionable in the 1880s for quilts and clothing. They continued popular in southeastern Pennsylvania through the early twentieth century, where quilters considered them perfect for appliqué backgrounds, a unique look. The chalky, pale green in the stripe, which looks at first to be from the Depression years, was also popular in the 1880s.

America's Printed Fabrics

Reproduction fabric. A good stash of shirtings is a necessity for reproduction quilts. Look for geometrics, stripes, grids, florets, and leaves in small figures with lots of white background showing through. Our definition of "white" is looser than that of the nineteenth century. Grounds today range from true white through ivory to tan, almost brown, or gray.

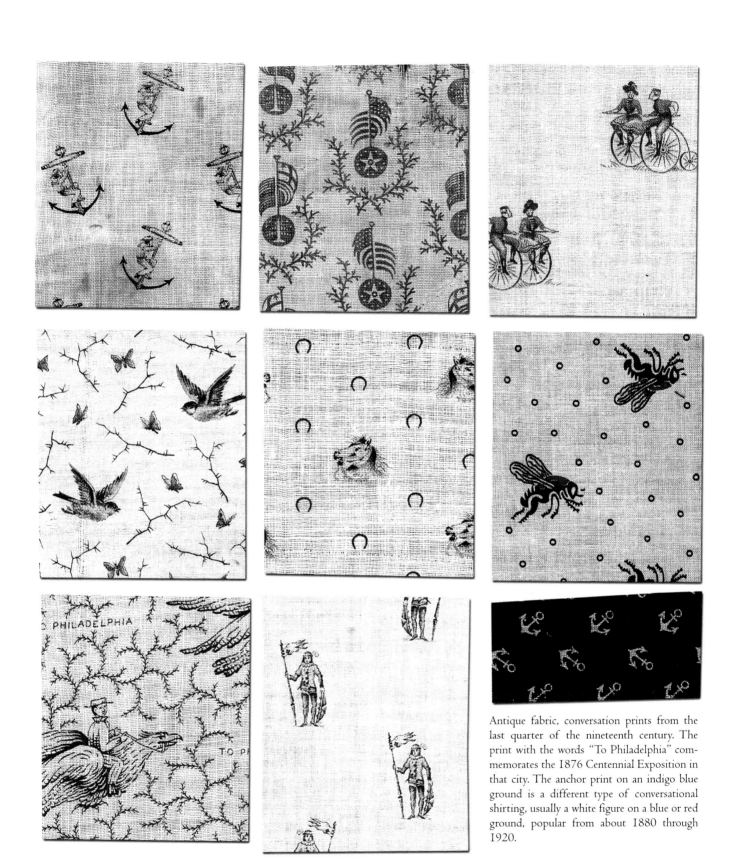

Antique fabric, conversation prints from the last quarter of the nineteenth century. The print with the words "To Philadelphia" commemorates the 1876 Centennial Exposition in that city. The anchor print on an indigo blue ground is a different type of conversational shirting, usually a white figure on a blue or red ground, popular from about 1880 through 1920.

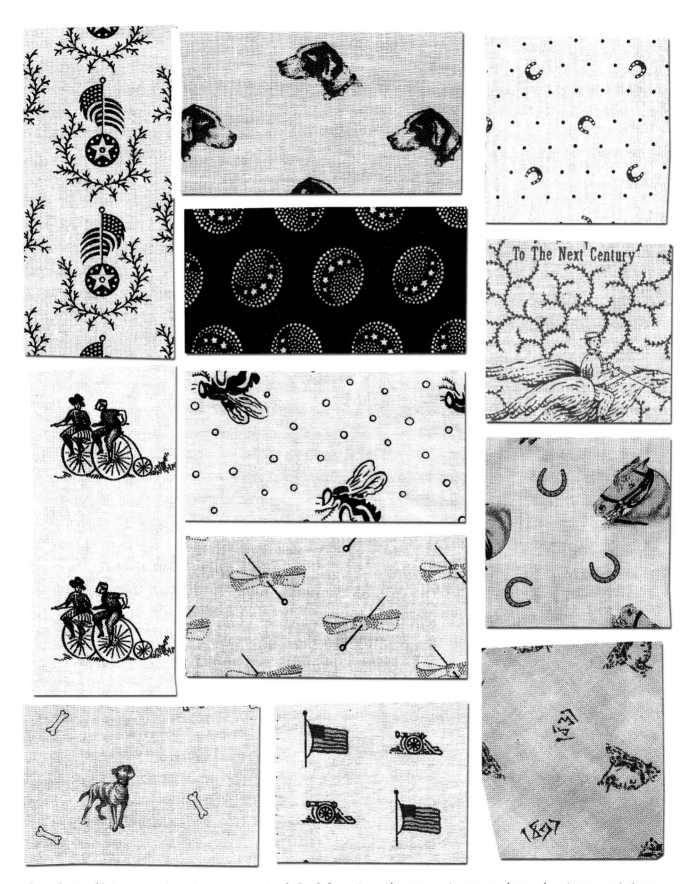

Reproduction fabric, conversation prints or conversationals. Look for sewing tools, sports equipment, cats, horses, dogs, insects, patriotic symbols, and human figures. The flag print at bottom center is drawn from a Civil War print. The Philadelphia print was reproduced as a millennial print for the year 2000. Don't forget the conversationals with white figures on blue or red grounds.

Lost Ship

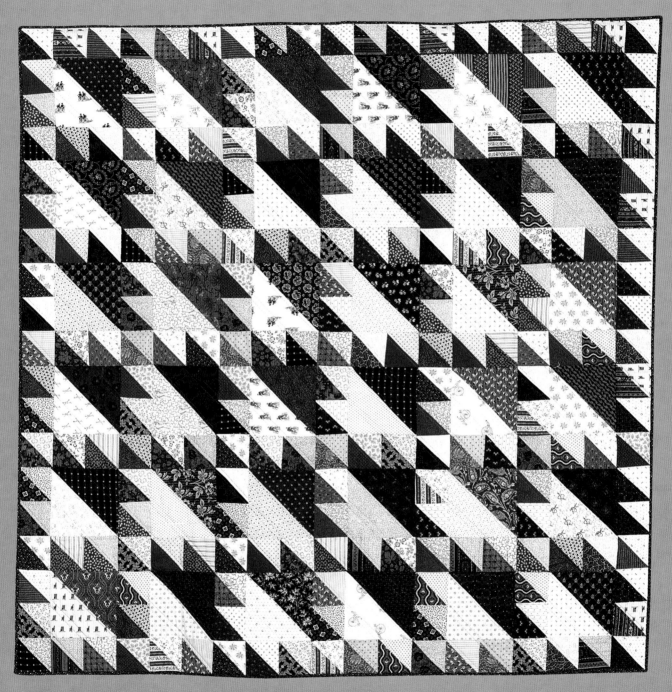

Reproduction quilt, *Lost Ship* by Barbara Brackman, 2002, Lawrence, Kansas, 57" x 57". Machine quilted by Pamela Mayfield.

This scrappy quilt captures the quiltmaking taste of the 1870s and 1880s with complex design and a palette of madder browns and shirting prints. The name originated late in the century with the Ladies' Art Company, the St. Louis pattern source for so many common quilt names. Dark "ships" catch our attention, lost ships in light shades disappear. The design is a tessellation. The ship shape, composed of triangles, repeats as the only design unit. A simple tessellated quilt uses only one piece, but tessellations also can be repeating design units composed of smaller patches. To finish out the design symmetrically, I added a border on two sides of the quilt only.

FINISHED QUILT, 57" X 57"   BLOCK, 9" X 9" FINISHED   BORDER, 3" FINISHED

FABRIC REQUIREMENTS

The look has to be scrappy so if you don't have a stash of reproduction madders and shirtings, buy quarter yards (fat quarters are fine). For the dark fabrics, look for reddish-browns, brownish-reds, and oranges the shade of a robin's breast. For the light fabrics, choose white or tan prints with small figures. Conversation prints with recognizable figures are always charming.

Dark madders: ¼ yard each of 9 fabrics
Light shirtings: ¼ yard each of 9 fabrics
Backing: 3½ yards
Batting: 61" x 61"
Dark Binding: ½ yard

THE QUILT TOP

I am giving you two modern methods for cutting and sewing. You may rotary cut each triangle and stitch them, or use the other method, which I call Triangle Factory, stitching then cutting.

METHOD 1. TRADITIONAL METHOD

Cutting

•Cut 1 square 6⅞" x 6⅞" from each of the 18 fabrics. Cut each in half diagonally (A). You will have 36 large dark and 36 large light triangles.

•Cut 109 squares 3⅞" x 3⅞" of darks and lights. Cut each in half diagonally (B). For blocks and border you need 217 small dark triangles and 217 small light triangles, leaving 1 extra triangle of each.

Blocks

1. For each block, sew a large light and a large dark triangle (A) into a square.

2. Sew 5 squares of randomly

chosen small dark and small light triangles (B).

3. Finish the block as shown.

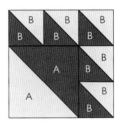

Block Layout

METHOD 2. TRIANGLE FACTORY

1. Cut large triangles (B) first, to be sure you have enough fabric. From your ¼ yards, cut squares about 8" x 8". Cut 28 light and 28 dark squares from your 18 prints.

2. Match these up, right sides together, into 28 pairs of lights and darks. Choose the fabrics for the pairs randomly to make the finished quilt look as scrappy as possible.

3. On the wrong side of the light fabric in each pair, mark a grid of 4 squares 3⅞" x 3⅞" each.

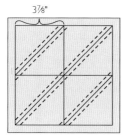

Cut on solid lines.

4. Mark diagonal lines on each. Use a clear, gridded ruler, or buy 3" finished triangle paper.

5. Machine stitch a seam on either side of that diagonal, ¼" away from the line.

6. Cut along the marked lines.

7. Press open each piece and you will have a square that is light on one half, dark on the other. You'll get 8 units per pair, more than enough for 36 blocks and the border on 2 sides.

8. For triangle (A), cut 18 squares of dark and 18 squares of light 6⅞" x 6⅞".

9. Make pairs of dark and light squares with right sides together. Choose the fabric randomly to make the finished quilt look as scrappy as possible. You'll have 18 pairs.

10. Mark a diagonal line on the wrong side of the light fabric in each pair.

11. Machine stitch a seam on either side of that diagonal, ¼" away from the line.

12. Cut on the line. Press open each piece and you will have a square that is light on one half, dark on the other. You'll have 36 units.

13. Throw all these squares into a bag and pull them out randomly as you sew the blocks, so you get the maximum scrappy effect.

14. Assemble each block as shown, using 5 squares of triangle (B) and 1 of triangle (A).

SETTING AND BORDER

1. Piece the blocks together into 6 strips of 6 blocks and press.

2. Join the strips and press.

3. If you turn the top so it matches the orientation in the photograph, you'll see that the design doesn't finish out on the left side and the bottom. The triangle border, made of leftover squares, goes on these 2 sides. Make a strip of 18 squares for the left border.

4. Add a strip of 19 squares for the bottom border.

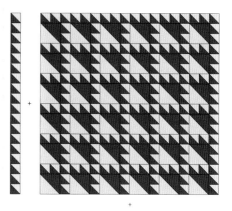

QUILTING

1. Layer and baste (page 125).

2. Pamela Mayfield machine quilted a traditional pattern of double diagonals across the face of the quilt. She used the patchwork to set up parallel lines ¼" apart with a space between the pairs of about 1⅝". This simple utility pattern is always a good period look for nineteenth-century reproductions and can be quilted by hand or machine. Double diagonals also make a good filler pattern behind fancy designs like wreaths.

3. Bind the quilt (page 126).

Triple Nine Patch

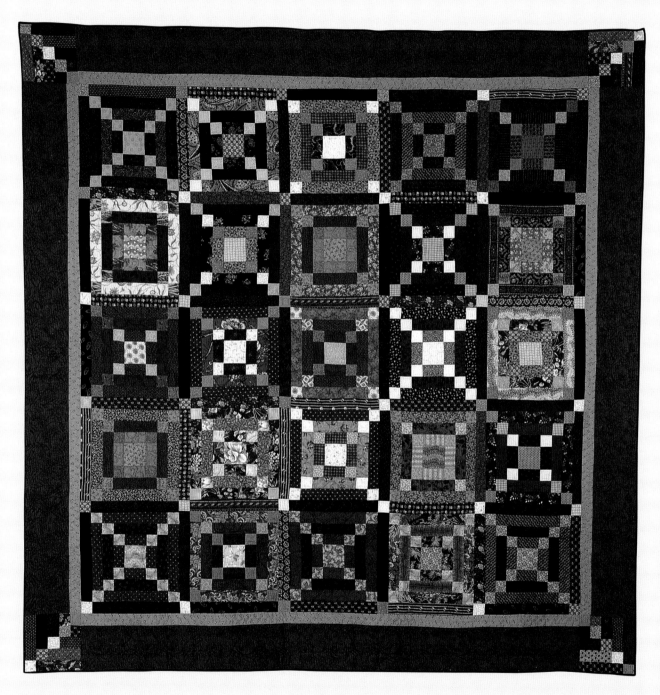

Triple Nine Patch by Barbara Brackman and friends, 2003, Lawrence, Kansas, 87" x 87". Machine quilted by Lori Kukuk. Nineteenth-century scrapbags were full of browns and pinks, remnants from everyday sewing. Girls wore pink, their mothers wore brown, up to the end of the century.

One way to get a really scrappy reproduction is to enlist your friends. I gave the nine women in our Sew Whatever group a pattern and a simple rule: "Pink in the squares, brown in the rectangles." I knew I wasn't in control. I used all their blocks, added a few of my own, sashed it, and finished up with a border. The block, a Nine-Patch inside a Nine-Patch inside another Nine-Patch, is of a type called a Single Irish Chain. The sashing and corner blocks complete the chain.

FINISHED QUILT, 87" X 87"

BLOCK, 12" X 12" FINISHED
OUTER BORDER, 7½" FINISHED

INNER BORDER, 1½" FINISHED

FABRIC REQUIREMENTS

Pinks: ¼ yard each of 4 to 8 fabrics (fat quarters are fine) of double pink reproductions, and ¾ yard (continuous) for the inner border.

Browns: ¼ yard each of 18 to 20 medium-to-dark brown fabrics, a total of 4½ yards, and 2¼ yards (continuous) for the outer border.

Backing: 7¾ yards

Batting: 91" x 91"

Binding: ¾ yard

CUTTING

•Cut 8 strips 2" x 42" from the largest piece of pink for the inner borders. Use the rest of this pink for squares.

•Cut 4 strips 8" x 69½" from the largest piece of brown for the outer border. Set aside to be added when the quilt top is

complete. Use the rest of this brown for rectangles and sashing.

For each block:

•Cut 3 squares 4" x 4" from different pinks. Cut into 2"x 2" squares (A). You need 3 sets of 2" pink squares (A).

•Cut I square 3½" x 3½" (B) from pink.

•Cut 2"-wide strips from several browns. From these strips, cut matching groups of 4 rectangles as follows:

4 rectangles 2" x 9½" (C)

4 rectangles 2" x 6½" (D)

4 rectangles 2" x 3½" (E)

Make 25 blocks.

•Cut 36 squares 2" x 2" from pink for the sashing squares.

•Cut 60 strips 2" x 12½" from brown for the sashing strips.

•Cut 20 squares 2" x 2" (A) from pink for all 4 corner blocks.

•Cut the following from brown for all 4 corner blocks:

8 squares 2" x 2" (A)

8 rectangles 2" x 3½" (E)

8 rectangles 2" x 5" (F)

8 rectangles 2" x 6½" (G)

THE QUILT TOP

Blocks

I. Add 2 rectangles (E) to opposite sides of square (B).

2. Sew 2 squares (A) to opposite sides of rectangle (E). Repeat. You will have 2 sets of A/E/A units. Assemble the Nine-Patch block as shown.

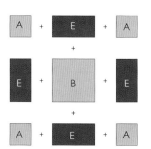

3. Add a round of D and A/D/A units and a round of C and A/C/A units in the same manner as Step 2. Make 25 blocks.

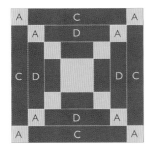

4. Make 5 rows of 5 blocks each by adding brown sashing strips between the blocks and stitching a brown sashing strip to the ends of each row. Press.

5. Piece sashing strips for between the 5 rows by joining 5 brown sashing strips with 6 pink squares, 5 strips and 6 squares per row. Press. Make 6 sashing strips.

6. Join the strips, alternating rows of blocks with sashing strips. Press.

Borders

1. Make 4 corner blocks by piecing a Four-Patch of pink and brown squares.

2. Add strips (E, F, and G) and squares (A) to this as shown.

Corner Block Layout

3. Diagonally piece the pairs of pink 2" x 42" strips. Trim to 69½". These form the side inner borders.

4. Piece the inner border strips to the outer border strips. Press.

5. Add the side borders. Press.

6. Piece a corner block to each end of the top and bottom borders. Press toward the border.

7. Add the top and bottom borders. Press.

QUILTING

1. Layer and baste (page 125).

2. Lori Kukuk machine-quilted a feather in the outer border and filled in the background behind the feathers by echoing 3 lines that followed the arcs of the feathers. In each pink square she quilted a curved line inside the straight seams. She treated brown rectangles as a large unified shape in which she quilted a feather wreath.

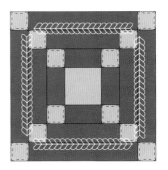

3. Bind the quilt (page 126).

Quilt Diagram

Triple Nine Patch

Reproduction quilt, *Thank You, Robert Bishop* by Georgann Eglinski, 2001, Lawrence, Kansas, 85" x 88". Machine quilted by Rosie Mayhew. For decades people who love old quilts have pored over Robert Bishop's books. Georgann made a very close copy of an antique quilt from his 1975 book *New Discoveries in American Quilts.*[16]

[1] Bess Beatty, *Alamance: The Holt Family and Industrialization in a North Carolina County 1837-1900* (Baton Rouge, Louisiana State University, 1999)

[2] Erma H. Kirkpatrick, "A Study of Alamance Plaids and Their Use in North Carolina Quilts," *Uncoverings 1988* (San Francisco: American Quilt Study Group, 1989) Pp. 45–56.

[3] Beatty, Pg. 125.

[4] Liles, Pp. 103-105. J.N. Liles, *The Art and Craft of Natural Dyeing* (Knoxville: University of Tennessee, 1991). Pp. 103-105.

[5] Liles, Pg. 105.

[6] Antonio Sansome, *The Printing of Cotton Fabrics* (Manchester: Heywood & Son, 1887) Pg. 26.

[7] Lewis Mumford, *The Brown Decades: A Study of the Arts in America* (New York: Harcourt, Brace & Co., 1931). *Webster's International Dictionary,* (Springfield, MA: G. & C. Merriam, 1938) Pg. 206.

[8] Harriet H. Robinson, *Loom and Spindle or Life Among the Early Mill Girls* (New York: T. Y. Crowell, 1898) Pg. 11.

[9] Simon Garfield, *Mauve: How One Man Invented A Color That Changed The World.* (New York: W. W. Norton, 2001) Pg. 65.

[10] Liles, Pg. 159.

[11] Quoted in Evelyn Leasher, *Letter from Washington, 1863-1865 by Lois Bryan Adams* (Detroit: Wayne State University, 1999) Pp. 191-192.

[12] Judy Nolte Lensink, *A Secret to be Buried: The Diary and Life of Emily Hawley Gillespie* (Iowa City: University of Iowa, 1989).

[13] Callcott, Pg. 341. Margaret Law Callcott, *Mistress of Riversdale: The Plantation Letters of Rosalie Stier Calvert, 1795-1821* (Baltimore: The Johns Hopkins University Press, 1991) Pg. 341.

[14] Rod Kiracofe and Mary Elizabeth Johnson, *The American Quilt* (New York: Random House, 1993) Fig. 168.

[15] J. Persoz, *Traite Theorique et Pratique de l'Impression des Tissus* (Paris: V. Masson, 1846).

[16] William Partridge, *A Practical Treatise on Dyeing Woolen, Cotton and Skein Silk* (New York, 1823) Pg. 143. *Transactions of the American Institute of the City of New York,* (New York: American Institute, 1864) Pg. 184.

Quiltmaking BASICS

Fabric requirements are based on a 42" width; many fabrics shrink when washed, and widths vary by manufacturer. In cutting instructions, strips are generally cut on the crosswise grain.

General Guidelines

SEAM ALLOWANCES

Use a ¼" seam allowance.

BORDERS

When border strips are to be cut on the crosswise grain, diagonally piece the strips together to achieve the needed lengths.

Butted Borders

Measure the quilt top through the center vertically. This will be the length to cut the side borders. Place pins at the centers of all four sides of the quilt top, as well as in the center of each side border strip. Pin the side borders to the quilt top, matching the center pins. Sew the borders to the quilt top and press.

Measure horizontally across the center of the quilt top including the side borders. This will be the length to cut the top and bottom borders. Repeat, pinning, sewing, and pressing.

BACKING

Make the backing a minimum of 2" larger than the quilt top on all sides. Prewash the fabric, and trim the selvages.

BATTING

The type of batting to use is a personal decision; consult your local quilt shop. For a reproduction look, choose a flatter batting with some cotton content. Cut batting approximately 2" larger on all sides than your quilt top.

LAYERING

Spread the backing wrong side up and tape the edges down with masking tape. (If you are working on carpet you can use T-pins to secure the backing to the carpet.) Center the batting on top, smoothing out any folds. Center the quilt top right side up on top of the batting and backing.

BASTING

If you plan to machine quilt, pin baste the quilt layers together with safety pins placed a minimum of 3"–4" apart. Begin basting in the center and move toward the edges first in vertical, then horizontal, rows.

If you plan to hand quilt, baste the layers together with thread using a long needle and light-colored thread. Knot one end of the thread. Using stitches approximately the length of the needle, begin in the center and move out toward the edges.

QUILTING

You may choose to quilt in-the-ditch, an updated look, echo the pieced or appliqué motifs, use patterns from quilting design books and stencils, or do your own free-motion quilting. Suggested quilting patterns are included in some of the projects.

BINDING

Double-Fold Straight-Grain Binding (French Fold)

Trim excess batting and backing from the quilt. If you want a ¼" finished binding, cut the strips 2¼" wide and piece together with a diagonal seam to make a continuous binding strip.

Press the seams open, then press the entire strip in half lengthwise with wrong sides together. With raw edges even, pin the binding to the edge of the quilt a few inches away from the corner, leaving the first few inches of the binding unattached. Start sewing, using a ¼" seam allowance.

Stop ¼" away from the first corner (see Step 1 illustration), backstitch one stitch. Lift the presser foot and needle. Rotate the quilt one quarter turn. Fold the binding at a right angle so it extends straight above the quilt (see Step 2 illustration). Then bring the binding strip down even with the edge of the quilt (see Step 3 illustration). Begin sewing at the folded edge.

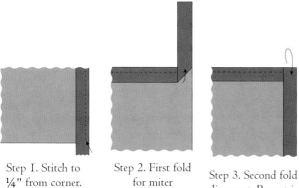

Step 1. Stitch to ¼" from corner.

Step 2. First fold for miter

Step 3. Second fold alignment. Repeat in the same manner at all corners.

Continuous Bias Binding

A continuous bias involves using the same square sliced in half diagonally but sewing the triangles together so that you continuously cut the marked strips. The same instructions can be used to cut bias for a vine. Cut the fabric for the bias binding or vine so it is a square. If yardage is ½ yard, cut an 18" square. Cut the square in half diagonally, creating two triangles.

Sew these triangles together as shown, using a ¼" seam allowance. Press the seam open.

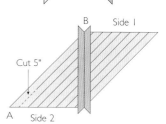

Using a ruler, mark the parallelogram with lines spaced the width you need to cut your bias (2¼"). Cut along the first line about 5".

Join Side 1 and Side 2 to form a tube. Line A will line up with the raw edge at B. This will allow the first line to be offset by one strip width. Pin the raw ends together, making sure that the lines match. Sew with a ¼" seam allowance. Press seams open.

Continue to cut along the marked line from the previous 5" cut.

Finishing the Binding

Fold under the beginning end of the binding strip ¼". Lay the ending binding strip over the beginning folded end. Continue stitching beyond the folded edge. Trim the excess binding. Fold the binding to the quilt back and hand stitch, mitering the corners.

Index

Resource List

Where to find full-sized patterns for the quilts noted with an asterisk (*).

Page 32, *Strippy Stars* is pattern #435 from Prairie Hands Patterns, 1801 Central Ave., Nebraska City, NE 68410, (402) 873-3846.

Page 73, *Antique Medallion* pattern is in the book *Twelfth Anniversary* by Gerry Kimmel Carr from Red Wagon, P.O. Box 520, Liberty, MO 64069, (816) 792-1540.

Page 113, *Centennial Block* pattern is in the book *Quilts and Stories From the Peace Creek Homestead* by Terry Clothier Thompson, Peace Creek Pattern Co., 15218 W. 83rd Terrace, Lenexa, KS 66219, (913) 310-0631.

The following quilt patterns are available from Sunflower Pattern Co-operative, the pattern company Barbara and Karla Menaugh own. Order from Sunflower at 5103 McGregor Drive, La Grange, KY 40031, (502) 222-2119.

Page 6, *Portrait of George Washington* is in the pattern *Daughter of the Revolution*

Page 10, *Princess Victoria's Feather*

Page 53, *Adam and Eve*

Page 64, *Prairie Sun*

Page 95, *Lee's Medallion*

Page 96, *Union Square*

About the Author

Barbara Brackman has written numerous books about quilts and quilt history, among them, *Quilts from the Civil War* and *Civil War Women* with C&T Publishing. She lives in Lawrence, Kansas, where she works as a consultant to museums such as the Kansas Museum of History and the Spencer Museum of Art at the University of Kansas. She is honored to be a member of the Quilters' Hall of Fame. With Terry Clothier Thompson, she designs reproduction fabrics for Moda. With Karla Menaugh, she publishes quilt patterns and booklets for the Sunflower Pattern Co-operative, and with her sister Jane Brackman, she publishes gift books about pets for Sirius Publishing. This book on nineteenth-century reproduction quilts and reproduction fabrics summarizes years of research she has shared in classes, curating, and in magazine articles.

Photo: John Gary Brown